D1542114

DEEP FAITH FOR DARK VALLEYS

DEEP FAITH FOR DARK VALLEYS

Jerry K. Rose

THOMAS NELSON PUBLISHERS
Nashville

Published in Nashville, Tennessee, by Thomas Nelson, Inc., and distributed in Canada by Lawson Falle, Ltd., Cambridge, Ontario.

Printed in the United States of America.

Unless otherwise noted, the Bible version used in this publication is THE NEW KING JAMES VERSION OF THE BIBLE. Copyright © 1979, 1980, 1982, Thomas Nelson, Inc., Publishers.

Scripture quotations marked TLB are from *The Living Bible* (Wheaton, Illinois: Tyndale House Publishers, 1971) and are used by permission.

Library of Congress Cataloging-in-Publication Data

Rose, Jerry K.
    Deep faith for dark valleys / by Jerry K. Rose.
       p. cm.
    Includes bibliographical references.
    ISBN 0-8407-3031-4
    1. Consolation. 2. Rose, Jerry K. I. Title.
BV4905.2.R68   1989   89–38753
248.8'6—dc20   CIP
        1 2 3 4 5 6 — 92 91 90 89

CONTENTS

Part 3: SURVIVAL FAITH

DEEP FAITH FOR DARK VALLEYS

Part 1
BEDROCK FAITH

1

THE LESSON OF THE NEGEV

The valleys also are covered with grain;
They shout for joy, they also sing
Psalm 65:13

My younger son Trevor and I went to the Holy Land and camped out in the Negev—that barren wasteland of Bible fame. The scenery was astonishing, with such variety from elevation to elevation that the sights defy description.

On the mountaintops, we looked for miles in all directions, drinking in fabulous vistas. We stood on the edge of the famous Sinai Desert where God gave Moses the Ten Commandments. Under the blazing Israeli sun, we climbed steep, ragged peaks, often hanging on by our fingers over the abyss—terrified to go on, yet knowing that we could not stop!

We couldn't stop because those mountaintops shared one sad characteristic. No matter how exciting the view, they were, for all practical purposes, dead. Oh, sure, there was some scruffy vegetation—a thorny shrub here and a brownish patch of withered grass there. But nothing to eat. Nothing to drink. Nothing to sustain life.

As beautiful as the view might be, we could not stay on the mountaintop. There was no future for us there. Had we stayed, we would have died of hunger, thirst, and exposure.

We had to return to the valley.

In the valleys of the Negev, the sights and sounds and smells were dramatically different from those on the mountaintop. Sloping deep into the earth, away from the mountains, the valleys were wonderfully cool, abundant with life. There we found the herbs that make superb tea, sweet berries with fantastic concentrations of vitamin C, plants that are used to make powerful medicines, thick growths of shady eucalyptus. We made our way down the canyon cliffs to a fresh supply of water at the bottom, where the agile ibex and other desert animals gathered to replenish their energies.

As we left the Holy Land, Trevor and I shared a new level of appreciation for the design of God's earth—in fact, for the design of our lives. The mountaintops are for thrills, but sooner or later, you have to learn the life-giving secrets of the spiritual valleys. Whether you face minor disappointments or major disasters you can learn the most during the low times of your life. The valleys are God's schoolrooms.

God's Schoolrooms

Running the vacuum sweeper, a mother comes across a stash of drug paraphernalia under her teenage daughter's bed.

THE LESSON OF THE NEGEV

Can she still trust God with her daughter's future?

A hard-working manager, with almost enough years to get his pension, finds a mass-produced office memo in his "In" box: The company is folding in three weeks.

Has God failed him? How will his faith hold up during these tough times?

Robert, the picture of health even at seventy-five, suddenly falls ill. Within days, a heart attack fells him, leaving behind a shattered widow who had not spent a night alone in fifty-six years.

How much good will her faith do her now?

A young lady is excited when she is offered the opportunity to teach the teenage girls Sunday school class. It is an answer to prayer for her. But within a few months, she is discouraged and ready to quit.

Has God's will changed? Was she wrong?

A broken marriage . . . a crushed career . . . the death of an infant . . . a brutal betrayal. Life in the valley can be difficult and sometimes deadeningly dull. How do you survive? How does your faith as a believer help you persevere on the journey when you seem to be surrounded by barren wasteland?

Bob had a good job that paid well, and he worked hard at being successful. The day the notice of the layoff was handed to him, he was stunned. He experienced every emotion—anger, fear, rejection, failure. His financial status presented a dilemma, but his greatest battle was spiritual. *Where is God in all this?* he asked himself. He had been a Christian for a few years and believed he was trusting the Lord. Where was God now?

Bob didn't find another job right away. In fact, two years passed before he went back to work full time. But the two years he was out of work became two of the greatest years of his life. "During those two years," Bob said, "I learned that God is the provider. Time after time when it looked as if I had reached the end of my financial rope, a check would arrive in the mail from someone that God had spoken to about our need. I discovered how independent and proud I was—too proud to want to accept any help from other members of the body of Christ. God helped me to understand how important it is to learn to receive as well as learn to give."

Bob learned that God can be trusted in the most difficult of circumstances. Bob's testimony, like the testimony of many others, is that some of his greatest spiritual growth was during the tough times. But most important, Bob didn't let the difficult circumstances push him away from God. Instead, he allowed them to draw him closer to the Lord.

The Secret of the Valleys

When Trevor and I camped in the Negev, we found a waterhole to swim in. Ice-cold water in the middle of the desert! But travelers in the desert have died because they didn't understand the secrets of the valley. When you learn the secrets, you discover that not only can you survive in the desert but the desert can be a friendly and wonderful place.

Faith brings you to that watering hole in the deepest valley and leads you to drink up whatever God has for you, then spurs you on to conquer another mountaintop. Faith, in fact, gets you through each day, including those countless, normal, everyday days, where most of your life is lived.

This book gives you more than a plan for survival. Instead, it offers you a plan to live a vibrant Christian life with a solid foundation. You can build spiritual character and develop a faith that will help you survive the difficult circumstances that will surely come your way.

This book is not about the classic mountaintop experiences that make exciting interviews on Christian television shows. This book is about the valleys—the places where all of us have found ourselves, more than once during the course of our walk with the Lord—the dark places, the sad places, the unpleasant places.

In the following pages, I'm going to take you into some of my valleys, and you're going to learn things about me that I'd rather nobody knew. But I feel that as I relive these experiences with you, you will learn the same lessons that the Lord taught me during those difficult times—life-changing lessons, valley lessons.

And I hope by the time you turn the final page, you will have something to take with you into your valley experiences: faith. Faith that will survive the storms. Faith that will outlast the longest trials. Faith that keeps the fire of Christ's love burning brightly within you, even when life seems its blandest.

You won't find heavy theology here—this is no textbook. It's a practical guidebook for everyday Christian living, because that's where I live. And I suspect that's where you live too.

In order to grow from where you are, you must know your faith. You must understand its makeup, where it comes from, and how it functions.

Begin by taking this short quiz on the facing page. Consider how you really feel about each of the following questions, not just what you think is the "proper" answer. Mark your answers. Later, you will take the quiz again to see if your responses have changed.

There are no scores in this "faith test." It simply serves as a tool to help you analyze where you stand in the process of building your faith. Probably no one can honestly answer "always" to all ten questions. But you can strive for a "perfect score."

In the thirty-three years I have been a Christian, I have come to see three distinct pillars of faith, which are vital to a successful Christian life: bedrock faith, where faith begins and upon which everything else is built; inspirational faith, where the thrill, the excitement, the motivation is; and survival faith, the combat zone where great battles are fought and great victories are won. Intimately linked together, these pillars become the bridge that supports the Christian's faith walk. Unfortunately, many Christians are not aware of these pillars, so when they experience personal struggles, they spiritually collapse under the pressure.

You will see how these three types of faith will keep you strong in the Lord, no matter what your circumstances. And you will have a healthy supply of deep faith for dark valleys.

THE LESSON OF THE NEGEV

	Always or very strongly	Sometimes or somewhat	Rarely or not much	Never or not at all
1. Do you believe in God?	☐	☐	☐	☐
2. Do you think you will go to heaven when you die?	☐	☐	☐	☐
3. Are you satisfied with your life?	☐	☐	☐	☐
4. Do you think God is satisfied with your life?	☐	☐	☐	☐
5. Can you tell when God is speaking to you?	☐	☐	☐	☐
6. Do you spend time daily in Bible study and prayer?	☐	☐	☐	☐
7. Do you believe your faith is strong enough?	☐	☐	☐	☐
8. Are you obedient to God?	☐	☐	☐	☐
9. Do you feel you are fulfilling God's will for your life?	☐	☐	☐	☐
10. Do you have total trust in God for every detail of your life?	☐	☐	☐	☐

2

BACK TO THE BEGINNING

I began to discover the origins of my own faith as a child, largely because my mother loved to tell me about my first life-crisis. It occurred long before I could even remember events, while I was still an infant in Terrell, Texas.

I was born in 1941 in my great-aunt's house. The delivery was normal, but I was not. My digestive system was dysfunctional. The doctor called the condition an upside-down stomach, but it was far more serious than such a name made it sound.

"There is no way we can save him," the doctor told my mother grimly. "There is nothing I can do."

I could not digest even the simplest foods. It was only a matter of time before I would die, literally, of starvation.

But my mother clung to her simple faith. She fervently prayed for her firstborn. My father, a good, solid, two-fisted fighter of a Texan, with a big heart and a quick temper, was not yet a Christian, but he did believe in the power of prayer. His own mother had been a praying woman. Now, with his infant son slowly dying, he was inclined to believe *strongly*.

I was six weeks old when I lapsed into a coma. When Mother saw what had happened, she screamed for Dad, her eyes streaming tears as she held my limp little body.

Cletus Baker, a family friend, was at the house, and she headed full speed down the street to the home of Mrs. Winnie Hennessey, a local "preacher-lady."

"Jerry's in a coma," Cletus told her. "Come pray for him!"

In moments the two women were running back to our house, already getting their prayer steam going. As she stood beside my crib, the "preacher-lady" laid her hands firmly on me and began to "call down heaven." She did not simply pray that I would snap out of the coma; she prayed for complete healing, absolute restoration of my sick internal system. Prayer was serious business with Winnie Hennessey, and when she prayed, people took notice of it.

Suddenly, my eyes opened. Mom picked me up and began to feed me, desperately hoping for a miracle. Cletus and Winnie went to their homes and continued to pray while Mom and Dad waited long, excruciating hours to know whether their prayers had been answered.

And the answer did come. Never before had a baby's dirty diaper been cause for such rejoicing. I had fully digested my food.

I was healed!

Mother frequently and joyfully recited that story for

me when I was young to instill in me an understanding of God's love, the power of prayer, and the importance of *faith*. She wanted me to realize that God loved and valued me. I was special, just as every person is special to Him. She wanted to help me establish a strong relationship with the One who created, loved, and cared for me, because she understood that our faith is based on relationship with our heavenly Father.

Unfashionable Faith

In any longstanding relationship, trust grows. Over the years my mother and others taught me that trusting God is the heart of faith. And this simple concept became the most important principle of my life. Bedrock faith—the solid foundation of faith—is trust in God.

You may be tempted to place your trust in government, doctors, educators, scientists, and pollsters. You may trust the economy to remain stable and the military to protect you. You may trust your marriage partner and your children to give you happiness.

Yes, you can enjoy having a reliable doctor or a happy family or a strong military. But in your heart, you must ultimately trust God, because the day may come when the doctor's knowledge runs short or temptation overtakes your spouse or the national defense lets down its guard.

Bedrock faith provides the firm foundation of knowing that God loves you, that He is guiding you, and that

He has given you the gift of eternal life, no matter what circumstances befall you. Nothing "shall be able to separate us from the love of God" (Rom. 8:39).

Bedrock faith has a distinctly old-fashioned flavor to it. You may have grown up going to a church where you heard numerous sermons on trust in God and were frequently urged to establish a personal relationship with the Lord Jesus Christ. And perhaps you've become so accustomed to the words, you'd like to hear a new message. But that old-fashioned teaching is on target. It comes from God's Word. It is God's design for you!

An abundance of the "designer theologies" have filled the Christian church and marketplace in the past several years and have all proven weak and ineffective. Every year someone comes up with a new revelation that sells books and takes the focus off the simplicity of the gospel. The church must come back to the basics of the gospel. Each person must have a personal, working, thriving relationship with the Lord Jesus Christ, God's Son. Nothing else does the job. Certainly, nothing else brings you into the presence of the Father at the end of your earthly life and ushers you into eternity with Him!

Nature teaches the meaning of bedrock faith. When construction workers build a skyscraper, they dig down through the soft earth, through harder and stronger layers of rock, until they reach bedrock. Bedrock does not break up or give way when pressure is applied to it. And upon this layer, construction workers settle the huge pylons that support the entire building—millions and millions of tons of concrete, steel, and glass.

Likewise, bedrock faith is established on the only solid substance in the universe, the character of God Almighty. Nothing shakes that supernatural bedrock, and nothing need shake you when your faith stands upon it!

The Strength from Rock Bottom

This unshakable faith is the only faith that will consistently withstand failure. Some of the popular theologies of the 1980s taught that "real" Christians couldn't fail, but were then found sorely lacking when Christians did fail! Failure, after all, is reality, a natural part of life for both Christians and non-Christians.

I've got good news, though. God does not reject failures. And He does sponsor flops. He even loves them.

Bedrock faith outlasts failure. Bedrock faith builds on the experience of failure. You can use the lessons learned back at the site of that failure to build a successful future. From time to time, I have to look back on the horizon of my past and search for those memories; I have to remember what God taught me in those dreary times when I failed. Bedrock faith takes you through failure, because you know that even in failure, God loves you.

Tom Peters, in his great book *Thriving on Chaos*, goes so far as to suggest that corporations should create environments that *encourage* failure.[1] The fear of failing can paralyze employees and keep them from accomplishing anything worthwhile. But employees who are willing to fail and secure in knowing that they will still have a job even if they do fail can attain new levels of excellence.

Bedrock faith is built on exactly the same concept. Your heavenly Father knows you will fail, but He will *never reject you* as He rejects your failure or your sin. He embraces you, He loves you, and He encourages you to try again and again and again. His divine character never changes. You can always rely on His faithful response to your failure.

This is the God I trust—the bedrock that I want to build my life and ministry on: a Father who lets me try and who lets me fail; then, who picks me up and teaches me and sends me off to try again.

Getting There

Getting to the point of believing in God's infinite love and having confidence that He is going to keep on loving you, even when you fail, can take time. It is not an overnight occurrence. Achieving a quality personal relationship with Jesus Christ can be a long and difficult process.

I've struggled with it myself for many years. From my youth, in spite of my mother's patient and godly input, I was quite insecure, and I tried desperately to mask my insecurities by playing the part of the "holy terror." I was incorrigible. If there was a fight in the classroom, I would be in the middle of it. Trouble followed me around like an ugly, loyal mutt.

One day some friends and I broke into a church to steal money from the soft drink machine. But a neighbor saw us and called the police. I saw the cruisers coming, and I hurdled through an open stained glass window, grabbing the frame as I swung to the outside. As my weight dragged on the frame, I heard a crack. I was really in trouble now: *I had broken one of God's windows!* But even a fear of God didn't slow me down for long; my goal was to put as much distance between me and the police as possible, and I succeeded temporarily.

My fellow paperboys and I often took time off from our early morning routes to sneak over the fence of the local swimming pool for a quick against-the-rules swim, then we'd hit the local pharmacy and steal pastries from the delivery man's truck parked outside. Great sport, if you don't get caught.

But finally, the owner of the pharmacy complained to the newspaper route manager. The manager was no Sherlock Holmes, but it didn't take him long to figure out who had pilfered the pastries.

He caught up with me as I finished my deliveries and confronted me with the charges. Figuring I was caught, I confessed.

"I've asked the police to keep an eye on you," he said, "and I intend to tell your parents."

I'm sure I turned a ghostly white. If he told my dad about my stealing, the story of my life would be a short story indeed. My father was an honest man; the word *stealing* was not in his vocabulary. He was also a big man, with huge hands and a long belt.

Who knows how I managed to pedal my bike home that day? Even as my jello-legs pushed the bicycle slowly up the road, my mind was racing. *How could I escape? How could I cover up? How would I survive the whipping?*

The phone rang as I walked through the kitchen door, and I knew it was too late. Dad picked up the receiver, and his face changed colors. "Jerry was caught stealing," he told my mother after he had hung up.

Mom looked at me, her eyes wide and sad, then turned back to the dishes in the sink. My grandmother, who was sitting at the table knitting, glanced up with a pained expression. I felt like I had been kicked in the stomach. How bad could it get?

I held my breath. My father straightened and walked toward me, his bulky form looking bigger than I ever remembered it.

I stepped back.

He raised his hand.

I cringed.

But instead of coming down on me, his hand moved up to cover his face. He sank into the chair behind him.

"Why?" he groaned. "A Rose doesn't steal." Then he mumbled, "My own son," as if the words were making him sick.

I gulped down the lump in my throat and looked up at Mom. She wiped her hands on the dish towel and sat down on the arm of Dad's chair.

"I reckon it was a childish prank, honey," she said gently. "We brought Jerry up better than that." Her gray eyes sparked a warning shot at me as she added, "And I suspect he'll never do it again."

"N—no, ma'am," I stammered. Mom's words and the pain written on both my parents' faces hurt more deeply than Dad's belt or Mom's switch ever could have.

In that moment I vowed to change. I would go straight. I was still only a young boy, but something profound hit home with me in that emotion-charged scene. I learned the hard way that my parents loved me, even when I failed them. But I realized that this unfailing love was not cheap or easy for them to give. It cost. It hurt them to love me when I failed them so miserably.

Somehow my eyes were opened to the value they placed on me, and as I realized my worth, I felt more secure. I could trust their love, which meant I had less need to mask my insecurities with youthful pranks or criminal activity.

I had not made a simple commitment. Full of self-doubt and entrenched in the habits of streetwise kids, I frequently failed in the years thereafter. But I always reached for the goal of integrity again: *I could trust my parents' love.* And their example would gradually help me understand how deeply I could trust in God's love. His acceptance of me was like bedrock—unshakable, unchanging.

Another Rose

It took another Rose, but not a member of our family, to lead me finally to that firm commitment of faith in God's unchanging love, a commitment to a personal relationship with Jesus Christ. This other Rose's name was Harry, and he led me, kicking and screaming, to the Lord.

Harry Rose was a young, enthusiastic pastor, who

came to our church when I was barely thirteen years old. He impressed me even then with his compassion for people, his commitment to Christ, and his infectious enthusiasm for the ministry. Harry Rose was different from the other preachers I had known. He didn't approach me or anyone as an authoritative adult to be obeyed. Consequently, I couldn't challenge him! I came to church with a chip on my shoulder, but Harry accepted both me and the chip and treated me as a friend.

When Harry talked about Jesus, his eyes lighted up. And through his sermons (as well as his personal example), Harry Rose introduced me to his Friend and Savior.

One Sunday evening, Harry brought me to attention.

"No matter what you've done," he declared from the pulpit, "Jesus loves you."

I was riveted. I had done plenty.

"He knows about everything we've ever done or thought, and He still loves us."

I squirmed in my seat. Mom had said the same things to me. But I could only think if God really knew everything I had done and thought, I was in big trouble.

"We've all sinned and done things we're sorry for," Harry continued. "But God guarantees eternal forgiveness and everlasting life. First John 1:9 reminds us that 'If we confess our sins, He is faithful and just to forgive us our sins and to cleanse us from all unrighteousness.'"

I was listening closely. Could God really forgive me that fast? I had done so many bad things! I had disappointed so many people, myself included. I didn't *want* to get into trouble; I sort of happened into it, as if something inside me just kept coming out. I didn't like myself that much; after all, there didn't seem to be much to like.

"There is one purpose in Christ's birth, teachings, crucifixion, and resurrection," Harry declared. "To save us! From the manger to the cross to the empty tomb, He came for us and for our salvation."

Harry thumped a finger on his open Bible. "God did not send His Son into the world to condemn it, but to save it!"

It was a classic explanation of salvation; I was transfixed.

"We believe by faith," Harry went on, his voice dropping to barely a whisper, "and faith is a gift from God. God gives faith so we can believe in Him. But there's more. Along with the gift, we are given the freedom to choose. That means we must decide who and what to believe and where to place our faith. For me, the decision came as I realized I only had two choices. I could either cast my lot with God or with Satan. I had been a rebel, going to church on Sunday and running wild the rest of the time. It didn't seem to be leading to much good. There had to be something better."

Sadness clouded his face, and for a moment I thought he was going to weep. Then the impact of his words hit me full force. *He was talking about me.* Tears sprang into my eyes; I fought them, but they came anyway. I swallowed with great gulps and tried to look casual as I wiped my sleeve across my face and slouched deep in the pew.

"One Sunday the apostle Paul reminded me of that

choice in his letter to the Romans," Harry went on. Then he read the passage in a loud voice. "'Don't you realize that you can choose your own master? You can choose sin (with death) or else obedience (with acquittal). The one to whom you offer yourself—He will take you and be your Master and you will be His slave!'"[2]

Harry looked out at the congregation.

"I chose Jesus," he said. "Won't you choose Him too?"

I could feel Harry's eyes on me, but I was looking at my knees. When I finally gathered the courage to look up, he had closed his eyes to pray.

I watched him for a minute. Harry loved Jesus and had accepted Him to be his Lord and Savior. Suddenly, I wanted more than anything to make Jesus part of my life. Tears came to my eyes again.

"Is there anyone here tonight," Harry asked softly, "who would like to ask God to forgive his sins and accept Jesus Christ as Lord and Savior of his life?"

My heart pulled me to my feet with an overwhelming desire for Jesus. It seemed to race ahead of me, down the aisle, dragging me along behind it. All my years of rebellious, stubborn arrogance dissolved as I felt the love of Jesus pour over me and His forgiveness cleanse me.

I had lowered the pylons of my life all the way to the bedrock. Now, finally, my resolve to be "better" would no longer be the flimsy resolve of a guilt-ridden little boy but the courage of a Christian, hand in hand with the Lord Jesus Christ, standing firm on the character of Almighty God—bedrock faith.

3

STORMS AROUND THE SKYSCRAPER

I wish that every story could end so well, but bedrock faith is continually challenged. You will find that you have to keep going back to that bedrock to remember where your faith was founded and to make yourself trust in God's character.

Sometimes as life rolls along, you become consumed with everyday activities and forget the basics. You slip away from that simple, old-fashioned trust in Jesus and begin to rely upon the trappings of life—career, possessions, health.

I had to learn the lesson of bedrock faith in a jarring new way almost two decades after I first accepted Christ.

I was called to ministry in 1974. After eleven years in the television industry, I finally received the opportunity I had so diligently prayed for: I went to work for a Christian television ministry.

As general manager of the Christian Broadcasting Network affiliate station in Dallas, I was content. I was managing a Christian station and occasionally cohosting the *700 Club* with Pat Robertson. Shirley and I lived in a comfortable house, close to family and friends. We were living the good life. On Saturdays we took our sailboat out on a nearby lake, and on Mondays I played tennis. My life was orderly. I wanted it to stay that way.

But that orderliness abruptly changed.

One morning, I walked into my office at the station and picked up the phone to place a call. Suddenly I couldn't see the numbers on the dial. My head began to pound, and I closed my eyes for a moment, massaging my temple with one hand. I looked back at the phone, but the vision in my right eye was partially obstructed by an ominous white haze.

Panic seized me. I staggered to my chair and dropped into it.

"What's happening to me?" I murmured.

I called out to the salesman whose office was next to mine. When he walked in, I could barely make out his features. I asked him to pray with me; then I told my secretary to call Shirley at home.

"Honey, something's wrong," I told her. "My vision is all hazy. You've got to take me to the doctor. I'm coming right home."

It never occurred to me that I shouldn't be driving. As I drove down the street, the pounding in my head intensified. I tried to read billboards and street signs, but they didn't make any sense. Words and phrases and meanings got twisted and distorted between my eye and my brain.

By God's grace I made it home, where I gladly gave up the driver's seat and let Shirley take control. As we approached the doctor's office, we passed a sign read-ing "Baylor Hospital." But as I read the words, they came out "Baylor Bears." Nothing made sense. I tried to tell Shirley that my head was hurting, but the words got mixed up as they spilled out.

"Hurt—Shirley—my—"

Shirley was horrified. "Don't try to talk anymore!" she pleaded. "Please, just rest."

At the clinic the doctor accomplished a short exami-nation and immediately sent us to a neurologist in the main hospital building. As Shirley and I walked into the building, I glanced at my watch and could make out the hands but couldn't figure out the time. In the eleva-tor, I reached out to press the button, but my finger was numb.

The neurologist examined me, testing my reflexes. Finally, he turned to me and spoke frankly.

"Your condition is serious," he said without emotion. "We'll have to put you in the hospital where we can keep an eye on you. As soon as you're admitted, we'll run a battery of tests and, hopefully, come up with an answer to what's happening to you."

I tried to talk, but again my mouth mixed up the mes-sage that my mind sent it.

Shirley came to my rescue. "Do you have any idea what's wrong?"

"Your husband has either suffered a stroke, or he may have a brain tumor," the neurologist replied. "We won't know for sure until we run these tests."

Fear raged in and through my senses like a forest fire burning out of control. My lips pressed against each other in silent agony while my mind shouted to God. *Oh, God! What's happening? Help me!*

But I felt no relief. I heard no answer.

The medical center housed the hospital as well as the doctor's office, so I was admitted immediately. The doctor began the testing with an electroencephalogram, or EEG. A machine with about twenty lines running to my scalp scanned my brain to detect any brainwave irregularities.

"Don't move; don't talk," the doctor instructed me. "Lie completely still."

I shuddered, then concentrated on quieting my body. This morning—so normal, so pleasant—seemed an eternity away. I wouldn't be sailing Saturday or playing tennis Monday. But I didn't think about such frivolous things for long. Silently I cried out, *God, I can't handle this! What's going to happen to me? I'm so afraid!*

My mind spun wildly back through scenes and dialogues I'd had over the past few days and weeks. Suddenly, I remembered a man's bandaged face. A woman had called the station during a television talk show and asked me to visit her husband in the hospital. I hadn't wanted to; after all, I was not a pastor and should not have to make house calls. But something down deep told me my attitude was wrong. So I went to visit the man.

Reluctantly, I walked in to the nurses' station and asked for the man.

"Are you sure you want to see him?" the nurse asked. "He won't even know you're there."

Now that I had made the effort, I was persistent.

"It doesn't matter," I insisted. "I'm a minister. I've been asked to visit him, and I really must see him."

The nurse shrugged. "O.K. He's in Room 410, down the hall to the left."

As I turned, I had to choke back the apprehension. In Room 410 a nearly naked man's body lay limp, lifeless, on the white hospital bed. Desperate blue eyes stared out of a face half hidden in bandages.

A tragic automobile accident had fractured his skull and left him paralyzed with irreversible brain damage.

I wished I had not come. I had never felt so inadequate as a minister. What could I say to this man whose ghastly condition repelled me?

God, I think You want me here, I prayed silently. *Now tell me what to say.*

The only answer I could discern from the scattered thoughts running through my head was, *Pray for him.*

I reached out to take his hand, expecting it to be limp. But instead, his fingers clasped around mine and tightened. I looked at his face, where his eyes flashed with panic and fear. They revealed the horror of a vital man trapped inside a corpse of dying flesh, unable to speak or move. He tried to speak, but there was nothing but silence.

I'm not sure how long I sat there before I was finally able to pray. Then, when it was over, I relaxed my hand, but he held on. His eyes were ablaze. I finally pried his fingers loose to escape and shivered as I walked away.

Now, as I lay on my back, unable to communicate and nearly blind, I saw his haunting eyes again, and the question nagged me, *Is that what I'll be like when this illness is finished with me?* In a frenzy of disconnected thoughts, I began to pray.

God, I don't know if I'm going to live or die or be a vegetable for the rest of my life, but I know You promised me I wouldn't be afraid. I can't cope with the fear.

And then, after I felt as though I had lain on that cold table for a hundred years, suspended between life and death, a gentle rush of words entered my mind, and the confusion began to drift away.

The LORD is my Shepherd; I shall not want. He makes me to lie down in green pastures; He leads me beside the still waters. He restores my soul.

The Twenty-third Psalm sweetly, slowly quieted my spirit. I let the words flow over me, bathing me in a peace that can only come from God.

Yea, though I walk through the valley of the shadow of death, I will fear no evil; for You are with me; Your rod and Your staff, they comfort me. You prepare a table before me in the presence of my enemies; You anoint my head with oil; my cup runs over.

Surely goodness and mercy shall follow me all the days of my life; and I will dwell in the house of the Lord forever.

I sighed; my body relaxed. I didn't know whether I would live or die. I didn't know if I would be physically or mentally impaired. But I did know that *Jesus loved me and I had eternal life.* I could trust Him, rest in Him, and He would take care of me. Nothing else was important. I had dug down to the bedrock, and I had something to stand on that was solid.

When the EEG was over, I said as best I could, "I . . . prayed . . . It's . . . O.K."

The doctor grunted an acknowledgment and continued reading the EEG results.

"You have a severe abnormality on the left side of your brain," he said, "with all of the signs of a brain tumor. Your condition is deteriorating rapidly."

But I was still enveloped in that calm, that peace.

As an orderly wheeled me in a wheelchair to my hospital room, I noticed a clock on the wall. "Shirley!" I cried out. "It's seven o'clock!"

I was thrilled. I could talk. My vision was returning. I could tell time!

That evening, one by one, the shattered fragments of my faculties reassembled themselves. Shirley was spending the night with me.

"I've called everyone," she said as she bent to kiss me. "The station has you on the prayer chain. Pat Robertson said he is praying for you. Harry Rose is coming to visit you."

I felt reassured to know that Christians all over the area were concerned and praying for me. But God had known my needs before the prayers had even begun, and He was already working a miracle in me.

The following morning, I felt tired but healthy. The doctor examined me and stroked his chin.

"I don't know what's happened," he said, "but the symptoms have vanished."

For the next few days, I went through a series of tests, all with negative results.

"You're a lucky man, Mr. Rose," the doctor advised. "Your EEG showed a considerable abnormality. Now we can't find anything."

But I wasn't puzzled at all. God had healed me. I had "walked through the valley of the shadow of death." At first I had given way to fear instead of holding fast to God's promises for strength and courage. But when I stood firm on the bedrock of my faith and placed my trust in God, that fear vanished and peace prevailed. Whether I lived or died no longer mattered. Only *Jesus* mattered. Everything else became unimportant compared to the value of my relationship with Christ.

My physical healing was not evidence that I had trusted God. In many cases, healing does not follow faith, because God for some reason chooses not to heal the physical body. But peace always follows faith. That feeling of calm, even in the storm, is the sure symptom of bedrock faith.

As you decide to trust in Him, to rest in Him, and to sink the pylons of your life down to the absolute bedrock, you will experience that peace—even in the darkest valleys, even when physical healing does not follow. Your peace begins with a knowledge of salvation—the realization that you have eternal life—and thus, the understanding that, ultimately, what happens to you in this life is not eternal; your circumstances here are not everlasting. The credo of bedrock faith is: *Regardless of what happens to me, I have eternal life. I can even face death, because I have a relationship with Jesus Christ!*

The Bible declares that nothing "shall be able to separate us from the love of God."[1] But we often fail to accept the literal truth of this promise. When you have Jesus Christ, you have hope in *every* situation because this life is nothing more than a "vapor" compared to eternity![2]

4

THE MASK-WEARERS

Do Christians not have problems? Does bedrock faith eliminate struggles? Not at all. This is not the design of the world where you live. Hosting the "Among Friends" talk show on TV–38 has demonstrated this to me over and over again.

I have interviewed evangelists, pastors, speakers, authors, missionaries, musicians—numerous people who serve the Lord in a variety of ways. But of all the people I have welcomed to the program, I have consistently found that the ones who make the most impact on viewers—the ones who bring the most *real help* to the folks at home—are the ones who are willing to be vulnerable, the ones who will admit to their struggles.

Sadly, plenty of Christians are mask-wearers—people who feel they must put on an act that communicates nonstop, trouble-free success. They have bought the Faith-Equals-Eternal-Success syndrome, in which they pretend everything is great, while they really feel devastated inside. Mask-wearers are not deliberately deceitful, but they have come to believe, wrongly, that being vulnerable or showing signs of struggle is somehow less than Christian. If we choose to believe this lie, we deny the premium Scripture puts on truthfulness, as well as cut our effectiveness as members of the body of Christ. I have a friend who claims he has never been discouraged. Not only am I unsure if I believe him, but I would never talk to him about my problems or disappointments because he probably couldn't understand. Although Christians do experience success, joy, good times, and win major battles against evil, victory is often born of pain or plain old hard work.

I spoke at a funeral for the nine-day-old daughter of a young preacher and his wife. The couple were sincere Christians, who wanted to present a Christ-like appearance to their relatives, some of whom were not believers. I watched as the young couple smiled and greeted friends and family with gracious words like, "Praise the Lord, our baby is in heaven. We just thank God for His presence." But every once in a while, they would let down their guard, and I could see the grief in their eyes and their gestures.

When I stood to speak, I said, "It's important for us to understand that faith is trust. Faith is trust in God, even when you hurt." I looked at the tiny casket and choked back my own tears.

"We know that this baby is in heaven," I continued. "But separation *is* painful. I want you to know *it's O.K. to hurt.* How we *feel* has nothing to do with our faith. It doesn't mean that we doubt God. You don't have to smile. You can cry and still have faith. Don't be ashamed to feel grief."

Relief spread across the faces of those bereaved young parents as the message took hold. And without shame or worry about what others might think, they openly grieved for their dead baby. Tears poured from their eyes. Jesus was still Lord, and their faith and trust in God was still intact. You do not have to put on a show. You do not have to perform. Jesus loves you, and you are saved. And you can be vulnerable.

Not Macho

You do not have to be macho to be a Christian. At some time you must straighten your shoulders, lift your head, and walk on in the face of disappointment. But there is a time for tears. You need only to look to Jesus as your example: Jesus wept when His friend Lazarus died, and He was "filled with sorrow" as He approached His own death.

Denying one's problems is not good religion, and it is bad mental hygiene, sometimes with devastating results. I heard of an active Christian wife and mother whose husband died but who refused to allow anyone to minister to her afterward. Instead, feeling that breaking down and openly mourning her loss would demonstrate a lack of faith in God, she kept a stiff upper lip and even tended those who came to the funeral. She quickly became active in the church again, always wearing a happy face. No one ever saw her shed a tear. Tragically, six months later, she took her infant son to the garage, climbed into the car, and asphyxiated both herself and the child. Perhaps if her friends had known, they could have helped. But she put on her mask and they never had a chance to help.

Everyone faces problems; this is a fact of life. Even the finest Christians catch cold and grow cranky and come up short of money at tax time. As the old saying goes, "There's one comforting thing about troubles; we all got 'em." The one thing we all do not have in common is *the way we react* to our problems. And this is where bedrock faith makes all the difference.

When we have bedrock faith, when we know we have a relationship with Jesus Christ and we have eternal life, difficult circumstances can help us grow stronger. God never intended us to be problem-free; He intended us to have problems that are *good* for us! "Count it all joy when you fall into various trials, knowing that the testing of your [bedrock] faith produces patience. But let patience have its perfect work, that you may be perfect and complete, lacking nothing" (James 1:2-4).

People do not like to hear that message. Face it: no one wants to suffer. Yet that passage offers more than a guarantee that Christians will suffer. James offers a beautiful hope that through suffering—*in our darkest valleys*—we can be assured of developing a maturity in our Christian walk. And that assurance is far more valuable than a few moments of ease!

I Love You When You're Bad

Vanessa, our only daughter, is my delight. One day when she was just three years old, she climbed onto my lap, cocked her head, and commenced a conversation that has stuck with me ever since.

"Daddy, I love you," she said sweetly.

I grinned at her, fairly bursting with fatherly pride. "I love you too."

"Why?" she demanded instantly.

I opened my mouth to say, "Because you're my daughter," but before the words came out, I realized this was not the only reason.

"Why, Daddy?" Vanessa asked again, growing impatient. "Why?"

"Well, I don't have a reason," I finally said. "I just do. I love you when you do good things and when you do things that are bad."

She eyed me suspiciously. "No you don't. You don't love me when I'm bad."

I was startled. Had I done something to make her question my love for her?

"It's true, Vanessa," I insisted. "I love you all the time. In fact, I can't stop loving you."

Vanessa digested this for a moment, then threw her arms around my neck and hugged me. Then, because I wanted to make sure she understood, we made up a bedtime song which we sang afterward for years:

> *I love you, I love you,*
> *I love you when you're good.*
> *I love you, I love you,*
> *I love you when you're bad.*
> *I love you, I love you,*
> *I love you when you're happy.*
> *I love you, I love you,*

Yes, I love you,
Love you when you're sad.

A silly song, perhaps, but an accurate reflection not only of how much I love Vanessa, but of how much God loves you and me. Whether you make good or bad choices, whether you feel happy or sad, God gives you constant, immeasurable, and unconditional love. Just as I cannot stop loving Vanessa—even when she has disobeyed me—God cannot stop loving you.

David, a man after God's own heart, wrote with clear and inspirational insight into God's character in Psalm 89:1, 2:

> *I will sing of the mercies of the LORD, forever;*
> *With my mouth will I make known*
> *Your faithfulness to all generations.*
> *For I have said,*
> *"Mercy shall be built up forever;*
> *Your faithfulness You shall establish in the very heavens."*

You may not deserve His never-ending devotion, and at times you may even reject it, just as children sometimes reject their parents' love. You may not always understand the depth of His love. But it is there—when you are grieving, when you are angry, when you are failing. God loves you. And He always will.

Here's the "Catch"

What is the "catch" to bedrock faith? Is the assurance of a relationship with Jesus all there is to it? The "catch" is that you must cultivate your relationship with Jesus Christ, because a relationship, like a living organism, will either grow or die. Our failures and our inclination to be neglectful can seriously dwarf the growth of our relationship with Christ. Bedrock faith has to be used and exercised;—it cannot remain static. This means you need to pursue a healthy process of prayer and Bible study—talking and listening to the One you are in relationship with, and witnessing—working the "faith muscle"—by sharing your Christ-relationship with others.

The Great Commandment in Matthew 22 is directly related to the Great Commission in Mark 16. Only when you have a dynamic relationship with God and man—as commanded in Matthew 22:37—can you really fulfill the activity commanded in the Great Commission. The two are inseparable.

While you can go through life feeling peaceful, resting in the knowledge that you have eternal life through a relationship with Jesus, you can only experience *fulfillment* as you *build* on that relationship. Bored, disgruntled Christians (we've all known a few of these) have found a place to take a nap and are simply waiting for heaven to claim them instead of building something valuable on the pylons of their faith.

You must hear God. You must stay tuned in to His voice and act on His direction. This is the next level of your faith walk: *inspirational faith.*

5

THE VOICE

I didn't hear a booming voice from the heavens. No angel wings fluttered down from heaven. I didn't see flashing lights or hear a celestial choir. I wasn't even doing anything spiritual like praying or meditating. But I knew it was God's call.

On one of those quiet, scorching summer days in Dallas, I was standing next to my mother at the kitchen sink, drying dishes. I looked out the window, mindlessly watching the feathery breeze tickle the tufts of Johnson grass growing alongside the porch.

I have a ministry for you.

The voicelike thought struck me with an intensity that brought my world to a standstill. My eyes locked into the swaying grass. One hand held a dish, the other a towel. Had I imagined it? But the words came again.

I have a ministry for you.

The message was strong, clear. God wanted to use me.

That moment of inspiration, that first experience with inspirational faith, utterly reshaped my life. I have never doubted God's call because I knew where the call came from. It grew out of my relationship with Jesus Christ. *Inspirational faith springs out of bedrock faith.*

Inspirational faith is not always dramatic, however. The prophets of the Old Testament often heard from God in a dramatic scene: Moses had his burning bush; Elijah dealt with an angel. And some folks have astonishing inspirational experiences even today. But because inspirational faith is simply *hearing God's voice*, it is, in most cases, an ordinary, everyday experience.

God may not have called you to become a pastor, missionary, or evangelist, but He has a ministry for you nonetheless. He may call you to teach or counsel, to serve in your church or community, or perhaps to pray for others. But whoever you are, whatever you do, God wants to use you, and He wants personally to speak His plan to you. He wants to inspire you to accomplish His complete plan for your life. That is inspirational faith.

Mighty Man of Valor

Gideon's experience of inspirational faith contains a powerful lesson still applicable today. He is one of my favorite Bible characters, if for no other reason than he seemed so ill-equipped for the task God called him to do and that is how I often feel.

In Judges 6:12 the angel of the Lord called out to Gideon, "The Lord is with you, you mighty man of valor." But Gideon, like many of us, could not believe that the Lord was with him. His list of problems was longer than most of ours. His country, Israel, had been oppressed for years. He lived in a war zone where, at any given moment, a band of marauders could descend on his family and massacre them. And to top it off, the country had fallen into spiritual disrepair. Israel's strong belief in God had waned as the people began to worship false gods and practice false religious rituals. In all likelihood, Gideon felt God would destroy Israel if the enemy didn't beat Him to it. The Bible paints a picture of Gideon as a frightened fugitive who meekly accepted his people's sinful lifestyle as well as the Midian occupation of his country.

Gideon saw himself, and perhaps rightly so, as a coward. Yet when Gideon asked, "If the LORD is with us, why then has all this happened to us?" (6:13), the Lord ignored Gideon's display of weakness and responded with an even greater challenge: "Go in this might of yours, and you shall save Israel from the hand of the Midianites. Have I not sent you?" (6:14).

Looking at the situation from Gideon's perspective, we can understand his reluctance. "How can I save Israel?" he asked. "My clan is the weakest in Manasseh, and I am the least in my father's house" (6:15).

Bible commentaries indicate that Gideon had an aristocratic background, so his modest claim is significant. He was terrified of being singled out as a leader; he felt insignificant and unqualified as a heroic deliverer. God saw what Gideon could be and what He could do for him, not simply what Gideon was. But Gideon wanted proof that the message was from God. He was not accustomed to hearing from God; he was not daily living in the realm of inspirational faith. You know well the story of the fleece Gideon put on the threshing floor in Judges 6:36–40. God patiently demonstrated to Gideon that He really was speaking to Gideon as He let the dew fall according to Gideon's request, one day on the fleece and the next day on the ground.

Gideon's first task as leader was to tear down the family altar of Baal. Instead of hailing Gideon a victor, the people wanted to kill him (6:30). Then, "all the Midianites, Amelekites, the people of the East, gathered together" against Israel (6:33). Although Gideon might have wanted to put his faith in the thirty-two-thousand-man army he had assembled (see Judges 7:2), God was not interested in a military victory. Instead, He was interested in teaching His people a lesson about hearing and trusting Him. So God told Gideon to send home the men who were "fearful and afraid" (7:3). Twenty-two thousand headed home. But it still was not enough.

God did not want anyone to think Israel had defeated the Midianites by their own strength. So he narrowed the troops to all but three hundred soldiers. Alone, Gideon might not have had the courage to continue, but by now he knew he had heard from God. He was living in the realm of inspirational faith. And Gideon's three hundred unarmed men went forward and conquered the vast Midian army (see Judges 7:6–25).

Gideon learned a valuable lesson and we can enjoy the fruits of his learning process without having to make his mistakes. Gideon saw his weakness—and even imagined a few extras—but he had the courage to allow God to use these weaknesses for God's glory. He heard from God, and he experienced the inspiration of the call: he experienced inspirational faith. Rather than depending on his human potential, he trusted in God's ability to work through him to accomplish exactly what God told him He would accomplish.

The Voice Channels

How does God speak if He does not use a dramatic, audible voice or messenger-angel? God has given us prayer and His Word as the primary channels by which He can speak to you and inspire His will in our hearts. By the faithful exercise of the same tools that form bedrock faith—prayer and Bible study—we experience inspirational faith.

Yes, we need preachers and teachers to break the Bread of Life to us. But we also need to examine the Scriptures and commune with God personally, individually, absorbing all we can on our own.

David plainly saw the value of this pursuit. He wrote:

Oh, the joys of those who do not follow evil men's advice, who do not hang around with sinners, scoffing at the things of God. But they delight in doing everything God wants them to, and day and night are always meditating on his laws and thinking about ways to follow Him more closely. They are like trees along a river bank bearing luscious fruit each season without fail.[1]

Jesus echoed this principle in John 8:31–32: "If you abide in My word, you are my disciples indeed, and you shall know the truth, and the truth shall make you free."

One of the most mundane but necessary lessons one must learn in life is "Read the directions." Perhaps you have discovered the hard way that assembling the bicycle or hooking up the new VCR is far simpler and much less time-consuming if you read the instruction sheet first. Likewise, God has given you a manual for life. The Bible is not an accent piece to be displayed on a coffee table and dusted once a week. It is meant to be opened, read, consumed, studied, pored over, digested, and acted upon. It is a workbook.

Prayer is communication with God, and, reduced to human terms, it can be considered a basic element of common courtesy. In any relationship, the parties talk and listen to each other. Yet many Christians go weeks or months without any talking or listening to the One with whom they are supposed to be the most intimate.

"Superficiality is the curse of our age," said Richard Foster in his book *Celebration of Discipline*.[2] This generation does not care much for depth; people like instant gratification and satisfaction. But Christians need to recognize this superficiality as a spiritual problem, not just a cultural one. Foster goes on to say, "The desperate need today is not for a greater number of intelligent people, or gifted people, but for deep people."[3]

This is also true, perhaps even more urgently so, in the body of Christ. Depth is not automatic; memorizing a few pet Scriptures to toss out at convenient times is not depth. Depth comes out of a daily relationship with Jesus Christ and an understanding of the whole counsel of God. Christians have failed to achieve spiritual depth for centuries. The apostle Paul sighed and observed,

You have been Christians a long time now, and you ought to be teaching others, but instead you have dropped back to the place where you need someone to teach you all over again the very first principles in God's Word. You are like babies who can drink only milk, not old enough for solid food. And when a person is still living on milk it shows he isn't very far along in the Christian life and doesn't know much about the difference between right and wrong.[4]

Study of God's Word is not an option; it is crucial in order to know God and learn the tone of His voice. You can't have inspirational faith if you don't study God's Word. If you claim to hear from God but don't study His Word, you likely are imagining things. The failure of many Christians to make Bible study a priority may largely be the fault of church leaders who have been inclined to want laypeople to turn to them for insights into God's Word. But this is not God's best for the Church. Even Jesus studied Scripture as seen in his frequent quoting of the Old Testament; He valued the Word. So God's best is for each believer to study and know His Word, spend quality time in prayer, and experience the challenge of biblical teaching as well as the joy of Christian fellowship.

No Mystery

Getting to know God is not a mysterious process; you get to know God in much the same way you get to know anyone. When I was getting to know my wife,

Shirley, we spent a lot of time together. We would walk, talk, and share our deepest secrets. Soon we knew each other well enough to know we wanted to spend the rest of our lives together. That kind of walking, talking, and sharing, essential to the building of our relationship with each other, is similar to the prayer and Bible study that are the means to our building a relationship with the Lord.

It takes discipline to make that daily date with the Lord. It is not glamorous; it is routine. But what sometimes may seem like drudgery pays off in wonderful, eternal dividends. Soon it becomes a part of your lifestyle. The daily sowing reaps a beautiful spiritual harvest.

You may not want to be reminded about Bible study and prayer because you are busy, involved with your family, career, school, or various other activities. Time is a precious commodity, and these disciplines take time. You expect your ministers and teachers to teach you. After all (you say to yourself), that is what they are there for! And that is true; the shepherds are there to teach and prepare the body for kingdom building, but you are a part of the process too. Your cooperation is vital.

Entire nations have made the mistake of depending solely upon their leaders for spiritual direction and paid dearly for the error. In Exodus 32 the people of Israel were left by Moses, who had gone up Mount Sinai to meet with God. The Israelites had neither seen nor heard from God or Moses in days.

The people had trusted Moses as much as they trusted God to lead them—a crucial error—and now that Moses had disappeared, they experienced a confidence crisis and panicked. Would he come back? Had God grown angry and smitten him dead? Had he lost his way or died of a heart attack? Who would hear from God for them? Wouldn't it be foolish to wait for him to return?

The Israelites went to their acting leader, Aaron, and demanded action: "Come, make us gods that shall go before us; for as for this Moses, the man who brought us up out of Egypt, we do not know what has become of him."[5]

The people had forgotten that God, not Moses, sent the plagues on Egypt and parted the Red Sea and engulfed the Egyptian army in the waters and provided the guiding pillar of fire by night and cloud by day.

Were they fools? Before you say yes, it might be wise to compare them to yourself. How often have you found yourself disappointed or defeated because you placed your trust in people instead of God? How many tragic moral failures in the lives of prominent Christian leaders will it take to drive you back to personal prayer and Bible study as a top priority in your life?

One of the major problems in the body of Christ today is personality dependence, almost personality worship. We can be easily charmed by people and come to depend upon them instead of the Lord. But we can be devastated when we take our eyes off Jesus.

Paul advised in 1 Corinthians 3:21, "Let no one glory in men." His warning sounds so simple we may not pay much attention to it. But failure to follow this scriptural advice can be deadly. At TV–38, as an expression of this principle, we instruct our counselors *not* to pray *for* callers but *with* them. I never want to be in the position of "answer man," the focus of someone's attention or trust as opposed to God's being their focus. Only Christ stands between God and man; He is our advocate. What we *can* do is hold each other's hands, unite our hearts in prayer and faith, and, believing, bombard heaven together. Anything beyond that can bring a false security in the individual doing the praying.

Part 2

INSPIRATIONAL FAITH

6

TUNING OUT, TUNING IN

After college I joined the U.S. Coast Guard Reserves. When I completed boot camp, I was assigned to sea duty on board a 311–foot cutter. While we were out on maneuvers, I visited the radio control center to watch the radioman in action. He sat in front of a complicated instrument panel, wearing a headset. Beeps, whistles, and cracks filled the air. I wondered how he could possibly understand any of the messages being sent with all the noise. What if a ship were in trouble or needed to send an important message? The safety of the entire crew depended on this fellow's being able to sort through the noise and tune in to the signals that would give the right orders and send us in the right direction.

"Isn't that rather frightening?" I asked the radioman. "With all of these messages coming through how can you tell which ones are for us?"

He smiled and replied confidently, "I have a trained ear."

Christians should be able to make the same statement. Today we are bombarded with messages from every possible direction. But in the midst of all the confusion we can hear God's voice, telling us the course He wants us to take.

Sources of Static

Do you know God's voice when you hear it? Or does it sound suspiciously similar to other voices you are hearing? Let's look at a few of those conflicting voices.

Friends. Sometimes God gives us friends who will be our wise counselors, but at other times friends, however well-meaning, can draw us away from God's message. Our friends' voices should confirm, not deny, what God is saying. In direct contradiction to what God had told Elijah, Obadiah tried to get Elijah to abandon his plan to visit Ahab. Obadiah was well-meaning but dead wrong.[1]

Family. Because they love us and do not want to see us stumble or fall or get hurt, family voices can advise us to be cautious. We must be sure it is God who is calling us to proceed with care.

Counselors. Pastors, business associates, bankers, lawyers—anyone in a position of authority can seem like an important voice to heed. But sometimes these people's messages are centered on human frailties instead of God's possibilities. We must be able to discern the difference.

Yourself. The voice we struggle with most often is our own voice, our own logic. We see our past failures and rationalize accordingly. "It couldn't have been God," we say to ourselves. "It was me and my lofty idealism. I'm not good enough to be used by God." Doesn't this sound like Gideon's initial reaction to God's call?

If you doubt that the voice you are hearing is really God's, perhaps this little self-quiz will help. Ask yourself each question, answer honestly, and discover the source of the voice.

1. Does the message conform to God's Word?
2. How are my own private preferences, motives, and ambitions influencing what I hear?
3. How emotional am I about this subject? Are my emotions figuring in too much?
4. Have I specifically asked God about this matter?
5. Will following this leading enhance my spiritual life or detract from it?
6. What do my godly counselors say?
7. Does this leading grow out of my own personal pattern of prayer, Bible study, my relationship with the Lord?
8. Who will benefit from this action: God's Kingdom or me?
9. Am I willing to do whatever God asks of me?

Keep in mind that there is nothing wrong with saying to God, "I'm confused. I don't have a clear picture. Please show me!" And there is nothing wrong with re-evaluating your decision after a time and admitting that you have made a mistake.

Hard to Get Out

A very close pastor friend of mine gave me some simple but profound advice years ago: "Stop worrying about God's will for your life." I was not sure what he meant, so he explained: "God wants His will for you even more than you want it. So if you want God's will for your life, it will be hard for you to get out of God's will because He will put barriers in your way and keep you in His will! Build your relationship with Christ, and the rest will fall into place."

That mini-message struck a chord deep within me, and I have had less problem finding God's will since that day. I have prayed fervently for God's will in my life and ministry; I have been deeply concerned that I was exactly following His perfect plan for my life and work; I have strained to hear His voice accurately on many occasions. But I have not worried. And you need not worry either. Your responsibility is simply to listen to Him as clearly as you can, obey as fully as you can, and trust His leading.

Jesus' brother James put it this way:

> If you want to know what God wants you to do, ask him, and he will gladly tell you, for he is always ready to give a bountiful supply of wisdom to all who ask him; he will not resent it. But when you ask him, be sure that you really expect him to tell you, for a doubtful mind will be unsettled as a wave of the sea that is driven and tossed by the wind.[2]

An automobile dealer enthusiastically advised me that he could get me a great price on a luxury vehicle. The car was nice and I didn't begrudge anyone having one, but I was reluctant because it seemed ostentatious. I serve in full-time high-profile Christian ministry and want to avoid an opportunity for the press to have a field day at my expense. But the friend insisted.

I talked with a few friends. They were either neutral or enthusiastic. I began to think perhaps I was making the proverbial mountain out of a molehill. I bought the car.

It was, as promised, a sensational automobile. But I didn't feel right. One voice within me insisted, *There's nothing wrong with this model. It's just a car; it's just metal on wheels.* But another voice countered, *It's also seen as a status symbol in our society, and to some it will be a stumbling block.*

A week after I received the car, I went to speak at a church. I didn't want to feel that I had to explain my flashy new vehicle to anyone, so I parked in the back of the parking lot. Finally, I went to the Lord in specific, insistent prayer.

"Lord, this is ridiculous! It's just a car. Several people have even said that as president of a television station, I deserve this. It's a presidential car. And besides, some of my minister friends have one. But for some reason I don't feel comfortable with it.

"I know there are ministers who drive luxury cars all the time. It doesn't bother them at all, and that's fine. But this bothers me, and I don't know what to do about it, because I now own it! So, Lord, please either help me feel comfortable with it or help me get rid of it. The car is not that important to me but doing your will is."

Exit One Luxury Vehicle

Within a few days of my prayer, I heard that my dealer friend had left his job because of the poor service the dealership was offering. My heart sank. It now seemed there really was no way to undo what had been done.

When I called my friend, he confirmed the news and told me how bad he felt about selling me the car and then leaving. "By the way," he said, "how do you like that Lincoln?"

I squirmed. "Well, Dick, to tell you the truth, I'm not really happy with it."

"But that's an incredible car!" he protested.

I started to give him a list of reasons I disliked the car—it was too big for Shirley, it was hard to park in tight places. But those weren't the reasons for my unhappiness.

"I just don't feel comfortable with it," I finally confessed.

"Well, Jerry, I'll take it back."

"How can you? You aren't working there anymore!"

"Don't worry about it," he responded. "Your old car is still on the lot. I'll take care of it."

By the following weekend, Dick had nullified my contract, and I was driving my old automobile again.

Driving a luxury model vehicle is by no means a sin. But the Lord had spoken something different to me; I couldn't do what others were advising. And though I had started down the wrong road, uncertain of God's voice, I had to obey His leading for me once I understood it, even if it meant embarrassing myself and changing direction in mid-course. Yes, it was "just a car." The model was not important at all. Yet, within the framework of my relationship to Jesus Christ, whether or not I kept the car was extremely important because nothing is worth losing my sensitivity to His voice.

When we become "hard of hearing" in our relationship with the Lord, we run grave risks. If I fail to hear, "Don't drive an expensive automobile," I will soon fail to hear, "Don't gossip" and "Don't lie" and then "Don't cheat on your mate." Indeed, rather than hearing less from the Lord, we should be hearing more. Thomas Kelley wrote in his classic book, *A Testament of Devotion*:

> God himself works in our souls, in their deepest depths, taking increasing control as we are progressively willing to be prepared for His wonder. We cease trying to make ourselves the dictators and God the listener, and become the joyful listeners to Him, the Master who does all things well.[3]

7

WITHOUT THE WIND

We may fail to hear God because we want to believe we can accomplish great things on our own. We may think we are spiritual enough to sense intuitively what needs to be done and then do it with our own spiritual strength. But we must depend on God's strength. The Lord used my wife, Shirley, to bring this fact home to me several years ago.

My friend, Gus, invited Shirley and me to sail with him and his wife on their new twenty-seven-foot sailboat, *The Sea Lady*. We were honored by the invitation. Gus had spent three years building her, and we were to crew her first voyage. On sailing day we approached the vessel, welcomed by her warm, flawless elegance, and her teakwood decks and railings.

As I examined Gus's excellent workmanship, I could not help but compare this queenly vessel to my own much plainer crafts. My first boat had been a fifteen-footer with a main sail and a jib—old, but steady. She made a sailor out of me. Later, I bought a sixteen-footer—a much nicer boat, though still shabby and insignificant next to *The Sea Lady*.

After we had cleared the harbor, sails full, we raced across the water. Gus shouted at me to take the helm. I grinned like a child at Christmas.

The wind whipped my face as I gloried in the power that I held in my hands. Shirley made her way to me, and I slipped an arm around her waist.

"Wouldn't it be great to own a boat like this?" I exulted. "She's the fastest thing on the water!"

Shirley grinned. "It is nice, Jerry," she replied, a twinkle in her eye. "But I thought a good sail depended on the wind, not the boat."

I was nonplussed. She was absolutely right. *The Sea Lady* might sail faster with her four sails up and full of wind than my little boat ever could. But when the wind died, *The Sea Lady* would be as dead in the water as any other boat. Every sailboat, no matter how beautifully built or how fabulously equipped, depends on the wind to sail.

In your walk with Christ, as you sail through life, you need the wind of the Lord's Spirit. As the wise sailor finds the wind and stays with it, the wise Christian finds the voice of the Lord and stays with it. Sadly I have known many well-equipped Christians with great talents and fine education who still accomplished very little for God. Like a sailboat without the wind, they could accomplish nothing for God with their power alone.

Beating the Guadalupe

Some years ago, Shirley and I took a trip to the Texas hill country to visit friends. While we were there, we decided it would be great fun to beat the Guadalupe. Surviving a trip in a rubber raft down the Guadalupe River, noted for its whitewater rapids, is considered a badge of honor by locals and tourists alike.

Before we had much of a chance to consider the dangers and change our minds, we were off. Our paddles were barely wet when the first rapids caught us in their chaotic turbulence. Walls of water drenched us and flooded the raft. We paddled furiously. My heart pounded above the deafening roar.

"The rock!" I shouted to Shirley. "On your left!" We slid sideways in the water, just in time to miss an elephant-sized boulder. We raced broadside through the churning white water—both the raft and our destiny, out of control.

Seconds later, the fury ended. The river's anger ebbed and settled into a gentle, pulsing current, and we floated along through some of the most beautiful scenery in the world. Shirley and I leaned back and grinned at each other, relaxed and proud that we had executed the first rapids in such fine form—more or less!

But after a few minutes, I could hear the faraway roar of rushing water. Shirley bolted upright and stared wide-eyed downriver. For a moment I wished we had never had this crazy idea. Then our survival instincts took over, and we grabbed our paddles.

White foam raged in and around the raft. "Keep away from the rocks!" I yelled, as if we could avoid them. But it was no use. The rapids took control again, bouncing and spinning us around among the rocks as if we were a miniature toy in an ocean storm.

Watery Grave

Suddenly, in the middle of a spin, I saw the end of the river. Ahead of us, the water rushed over a cliff, and from the ferocious roar, I could tell it was at least twenty feet high. There was no escape. We approached the fall, the water beneath us lunging for the edge, jerking the helpless raft to the precipice. We held the raft tightly as we faced our watery grave.

Only a second later, we landed upright, still seated on our raft, floating gently along. Exhausted and exhilarated, I looked back to see the mammoth waterfall we had survived. It was well over two feet high!

I swallowed a chuckle as we paddled ashore for a picnic lunch—what pioneers! It felt great to put my feet on the ground again and to be back in control. But I realized that God was leading us through an outdoor object lesson. In life, we can feel as if we are in calm water one moment and raging whitewater rapids the next. And some problems we encounter are like the waterfalls I saw—they look a lot bigger as we approach them than they do after we have passed through them.

Despite this realization, I knew the Guadalupe wasn't through with us, and as we ate lunch, I thought about other routes back to our car. We had parked downriver a few miles. The most logical way to reach the car would be to follow the river. But that would mean experiencing everything the river offered—the fury of the rapids, the treacherous falls, spelled only occasionally by serene stretches of stillness. And if we walked, we would have to combat thick underbrush, dark woods, sheer cliffs. We could easily get lost in the rugged terrain.

I quickly decided that even though the trip might be rough, it was better to stay with the river. We knew the river would flow by our car. It had been cutting the same path through this mountain for centuries. If we submitted ourselves to the river, it would take us to our destination, and we wouldn't get lost.

Submit to the River

The river was by now a twisting, turning, bubbling source of inspiration to me. Like the voice of God's Spirit, the river was calling us, beckoning us to go with the flow. You can depend on God for your destination; the current of His will flows in the direction you need to go. He is absolute, consistent, forever. And there is no waterfall too high, no rapids too treacherous, for Him to control. "Trust in the LORD with all your heart," Proverbs 3:5 recommends, "and do not rely on your own insight. In all your ways acknowledge him, and he will make straight your paths."

God's way is not always smooth, but it is always the best way. It is always the right way. And it always leads to the destination He has divinely appointed for us, so we must learn to hear God's voice and follow the river.

In order to submit to the river, we must die to our own selfish preferences. And though submission runs contrary to the desires of our flesh, we must endure this painful process if we are to experience the good God has in store for us. "Self is the only prison that can ever bind the soul," Henry Van Dyke rightly declared.

The apostle Paul wrapped up this concept into a single power-packed verse of Scripture, Romans 12:1: "I beseech you, _____ [insert your own name here], to present your body as a living sacrifice, holy, acceptable to God, which is your reasonable service."

Paul called us to quit demanding our way—that is the "living sacrifice" part. God is pleased with that act of submission: He calls it "holy." Paul then describes that submission as "reasonable service." The Greek word translated *reasonable* embodies other meanings as well: logical, rational, but also spiritual.

God's plan will be accomplished in our lives if we continually submit to Him.

Too Good to Be Prayed About

The river of God's will does not necessarily lead you to your destination on your schedule. God's timing can be surprising—even frustrating. And the timetable you desire makes it all the more important to *hear God's voice*.

After working in commercial television and radio for nine long years, I was anxious to move into Christian work, knowing this was God's calling in my life. When an advertising agency for the Southern Baptists posted an opening for an executive producer, I was sure I was the guy for the job—so sure that I did not even bother to make it a matter of prayer. I packed up my portfolio and set out with great enthusiasm for my interview. I went from office to office, selling myself with great aplomb. Everyone seemed impressed. The only detail they could not find on my long résumé was experience with film budgeting, but they agreed with me when I insisted I was a fast study. The head of the agency assured me that I could very well be the man for the job, and I would hear from them in a couple of weeks.

I soared out of the interview, confident that in a few short weeks, the job would be mine. Those nine endless years of waiting, praying, and learning would finally pay off. This must be God's will—Christian communications at last.

I raced back to the station where I was working and stopped for a cup of coffee with my coworker Wayne. I couldn't wait to tell him my great news.

"Hey, man, I'm really happy for you," Wayne responded warmly, grinning with me. "Congratulations!"

A few days later, another staff member stopped me in the hall. There was gossip in the air.

"Did you hear Wayne is leaving?" he asked.

"No!" I answered. "Where is he going?"

"He's going to be executive producer for the Southern Baptists," he replied casually and walked on.

Stunned, I stood in the corridor. I couldn't move; I couldn't believe it. I was devastated. Hurt, disillusioned, and bitter. Deeply bitter. Without realizing what was happening, I began to harbor strong resentment.

I couldn't get it out of my mind. "That job should have been mine," I growled. "God knows it and I know it. Those people just weren't listening to God." Every time the incident came to mind, which was plenty often, I flushed with anger and spouted out my frustration to anyone who happened to be within earshot, usually to Shirley.

But my anger could not last forever. Shirley saw to that. One day as we drove down a Dallas freeway, she interrupted my grousing.

"I wish you'd be quiet," she said, eyes flashing.

I was shocked. "What are you talking about?"

"You! You and that—job!" Then began her slashing lecture. "You go to church, you're always reminding people about Romans 8:28—that 'all things work together for good to those who love God.' You preach it, but you don't live it."

"Of course, I do," I stammered.

"No, you don't," she hit back. "If you practiced what you preached, you wouldn't be complaining so much. Don't you see? If this job had been God's will for you, you would have gotten it."

I gulped. My face burned with anger, then with shame.

"You're right," I admitted quietly. "You're absolutely right."

Besides acting like a spoiled child, I had tried to commandeer God's will into my own timetable because I had failed to listen for God's voice.

I wish I had really understood at the time; it could have saved me some pain. God had not forgotten me. His plan was steadily unfolding in my life.

It was not long before the Lord steered me to Habakkuk 2:3 (TLB), "These things I plan won't happen right away. Slowly, steadily, surely, the time approaches when the vision will be fulfilled. If it seems slow, do not despair, for these things will surely come to pass. Just be patient! They will not be overdue a single day!"

No one hurries—or slows—the Lord.

8

THE ISAAC DREAM

Many Christians make the mistake of valuing their ministry more than God's will; they fail to realize that the two may not be synonymous. In the many years before I finally got into Christian television, I would lie awake nights, crying out to God: *When are you going to put me in full-time ministry? When is the door going to open?*

But one night the Lord opened my eyes to my error. I had come to place more value on "my ministry" than on His will! In fact, the Lord challenged me with a question: *Are you willing to give up full-time ministry and stay in commercial television, if that's My will for your life? What if I want your ministry to be in commercial television? What if I want you to spend the rest of your life doing exactly what you're doing now? Are you willing?*

I was stunned by the thought. But I had to admit I had come to imagine Christian television as glamorous and comfortable. I longed for the workplace where people talked openly about the things of the Lord, a place where people walked around saying, "Praise the Lord!" Full-time ministry had almost become my obsession.

The commercial television industry was a difficult place to be a Christian. Temptations lurked around every corner. Many of the programs on commercial stations depicted lust and violence. I wanted to get away from all that. In my mind, moving into Christian television would have been like walking from the ghetto into the Garden of Eden—it would be a safe and pleasant haven.

Was God now making an "Isaac" out of my dream? Was He asking me to put my ministry on the altar and sacrifice it to Him?

Finally, I relented. "Yes, Lord, if you want me to stay in commercial television, I'll stay."

Instead of the grief I expected, I felt relief. I had experienced inspirational faith, and in an instant, the pressure to escape commercial television vanished. I was at peace because my future was in God's hands.

Just Like Schweitzer

Inspirational faith has to be a continuing process, not a momentary event. Within a few months, I was pressing ahead of God's timetable again.

What about missionary service? I wondered. To me, this was a high calling; my high-school heroes were the medical colossus Albert Schweitzer and the famous Pentecostal missionary, Charles Greenaway. The idea of "giving up everything" to go to a primitive land to spread the gospel and help people in need was appealing.

THE ISAAC DREAM

I had some ideas of how I could use my skills in missions, so I tried them out on two veteran missionaries—Del Kingswriter, who was involved in missions work in Africa, and Dr. George Flattery, the founding president of International Correspondence Institute in Brussels. I wanted to launch an international communications division of their denomination—an operation that would support missionaries by helping meet their communications needs.

First, we would form drama and music teams to evangelize. These teams would travel from village to village, conducting street dramas and concerts. Second, teaching teams would move in to teach and assist new converts in their Christian growth. Those with leadership abilities and a desire to serve would be sent to Bible colleges. After their education, they would return to their own areas as pastors and evangelists. We would also work with foreign governments to secure air time for Christian programming on local radio and television stations.

Both men warmed to the plan, and they presented it to the leadership of their mission board. All agreed that this was the time to implement such an idea, and they sent me an application for foreign missionary service, which Shirley and I promptly filled out.

All of this action suggested to me that God was really moving. *We're right on target*, I told myself. Still, down deep inside me, there was something wrong. I did not have complete peace about the missions position, but I kept putting all those feelings beneath the surface.

Then one morning in 1973, the phone call that I had

waited to receive for more than a decade came. Pat Robertson, founder of the Christian Broadcasting Network, was on the other end of the line. He had heard about me from a number of pastors and television people in the Dallas area. I came highly recommended, he said.

"The reason I'm calling is that I want to put an affiliate station on the air in Dallas," Pat said, "and I would like you to head up the project."

I inhaled sharply. *No way*, I thought. *It's the mission field for me.*

Change of Plan

"I can't," I responded firmly. "I'm going to the mission field." I told him the plan for an overseas communications ministry.

"Brother," he chuckled ruefully, "you're going to be knocking on hundreds of church doors, trying to get them to support you and your family in Africa. It will be months before you have enough money. I'm talking about starting the station *now*."

We talked for a while. I stayed with the conversation mostly out of courtesy. Finally, he tried another tack: "Why don't you stay long enough to get the station going? Then, if you still want to go into missions, no problem."

This, I thought, might be workable. I suggested some conditions: CBN would have to match my current salary, give me the freedom to preach and gather support in the evenings, and promise to support me on the mission field.

THE ISAAC DREAM

Pat Robertson agreed. It was settled. I had my dream job in hand, and in a few months, when Shirley and I were ready to go to Africa, I would have CBN's considerable financial support.

But that night I awoke out of a sound sleep, sweating. I sat up in bed, fully awake. I heard a voice in my spirit—the same voice that I had heard as I stood at my mother's kitchen sink so many years before: *No, I don't want you to go to the mission field.*

It couldn't be God. Surely God wouldn't tell me *not* to go to the mission field. *If this is really you, God,* I prayed, *please show me.*

I lay back down and tried to block out the message so I could go back to sleep. But the more I tried, the more it haunted me.

I restlessly chewed over the matter the next day and, after work, came to Shirley in the kitchen. I told her about the leading I had received the night before and the turmoil I had suffered all day.

"We have to pray about this," I said, leading her by the elbow. "I intend to stay on my knees until I get an answer."

I expected her to be surprised, but she was, instead, at ease.

"I've got to know," I urged her.

"We both do," she answered. She took my hand, and together we went to our room.

On our knees, side by side, we prayed and wept and felt the Lord's overwhelming love sweep over us. After an hour, we had our answer.

"I don't think God wants us to go to Africa," I told her.

"I got the same message," Shirley replied. "But we are going to Dallas."

"Yeah," I said, but already I was thinking of my pride. I do not like being wrong, and I hate having to admit it, especially to the venerable leadership of my denomination's mission board.

What would I say to them? I thought of all the time and effort and money that they had already invested in this venture.

"Just tell the truth," Shirley advised. "That's all we really can do."

I then wrote the most difficult letter I have ever written.

I figured the board would think I was flaky, a nut, and would have nothing more to do with me. And even though I was sure God did not want me to go to Africa, I felt guilty. Dallas and a nice office, an ample salary, a comfortable home; it all seemed too good, too comfortable. What would replace all the blood, sweat, and tears I could have shed in Africa for the cause of Christ? That would have been noble; that would have been a sacrifice.

But God would not let me wallow in my error. *I did not ask you to sacrifice*, He spoke to my heart. *I asked you to obey.* The words of 1 Samuel 15:22 stung me: "Has the LORD as great delight in burnt offerings and sacrifices, / As in obeying the voice of the LORD? / Behold, to obey is better than sacrifice, / And to heed than the fat of rams."

As I now look back on that situation, I smile. Had I known of the sacrifices I would have to make here in the

States and how difficult the task of working in Christian television would be, I might have regarded darkest Africa as the more plush and comfortable place to be. Yet out of that experience I came to realize that my idea of ministry is not always God's will for me; my preferences are not necessarily His best for me.

God's view of you is often different from your view of yourself. You must stay tuned in to His voice in order to keep His perspective. You may see yourself in an active, high-profile ministry; God may see you in the background. You may feel you have little to offer; God may see you as a dynamic leader. How will you know? Learn to hear God's voice and obey what He tells you.

God's plan for you, like the twisting, raging Guadalupe River, may take you through wildly varying situations. God led me through a frustrating decade of work in commercial television. Why? As it turns out, that experience precisely prepared me for the ministry He intended me to have later. In countless unlikely settings—spinning jazz records in the middle of the night, running TV cameras and designing sets—He was planting in me the skills and abilities to handle the tasks He would assign to me later. By the time the board of TV–38 asked me to assume the presidency of the station, I knew God had made me ready.

Hear God's voice. Submit to the river. God's plan for you will be an exciting lifetime journey!

9

OBADIAH'S ADVICE

Inspirational faith requires action. "Faith without works is dead," James 1:26 declares. Remember the story about Gideon? Once he heard from God, he had to act on that word. And once you hear from God, you must likewise act on that word—even when circumstances defy you.

In the Old Testament we read the story of the prophet Elijah, who got stuck in a tough situation. The earth was dry from drought, and God told Elijah to visit King Ahab; then, He would send rain. But Ahab was a vile creature who had sworn to murder the prophet.

Elijah's friend and fellow prophet, Obadiah, advised his colleague strongly against going to the palace. (See 1 Kings 18). But Elijah knew God's voice and had learned to sort through the static. Remembering God's word to him, Elijah ignored his friend's advice, went to Ahab, and lived to see the rain fall.

Through the years, I have learned the lesson of acting on inspirational faith in a variety of ways, but never more vividly than when the Lord called me to Chicago. I was working at Christian Broadcasting Network (CBN) in Virginia in 1975, serving as the operations director for the network, when I received a call from Owen Carr, a name I recognized. Rumor had pegged Owen as the unrealistic pastor of the famous Stone Church, who was trying to launch a Christian television station in Chicago. The board of directors wanted me to help them put a new full-time Christian television station on the air.

"We'd like you to join our team as president of the corporation," he said.

I was flattered, but leery. "Where do you stand at this point?"

"I'm afraid we haven't gotten very far."

"How is your financial situation?"

"Well, we don't have much money."

"What about personnel? I assume you have people with experience in television."

"No," Owen chuckled. "In fact, I barely know where to find the on and off switch on my set at home."

"You have a license?"

"No."

"A transmitter?"

"No."

"Well, what do you have?"

"Faith," Owen said plainly. "We believe God wants it to happen. Right now we're trying to make a deal with the Chicago Federation of Labor for an open channel they want to sell. Channel 38 has never been on the air. I've negotiated the labor union down from five million to just one million. Now we just have to raise the money.

Jerry, all we really have right now is faith and $25,000 in escrow."

I sighed. "Well, Owen, I hope it all works out," I felt almost hypocritical for encouraging such a kamikaze mission, "but I really can't accept your offer. Maybe I can put you in touch with someone else."

Moments later, as I hung up, I happened to remember a request I had made to God years before: *Lord, I'll do anything you want and go anywhere you want me to go, but whatever you do, please don't send me to New York, Los Angeles, or Chicago.* I did not want to have anything to do with these three centers of commercial television.

The Land of Al Capone

Chicago, especially, seemed like an unpleasant location. I thought of it as an austere, frigid-in-the-winter, sweltering-in-the-summer city that spawned the likes of Al Capone. I had only visited Chicago once as a thirteen-year-old, when my family drove up north for a vacation. Our friends had warned us about the "dangerous city." "Don't get out of your car," they told us, "or you'll get your pockets picked." With their words still on our minds, we drove into the city, all the way to Lake Michigan, and then turned around and drove back out again, without ever getting out of the car.

Another time I worked for an ABC "Wide World of Sports" event in Johnston City, Illinois—the World Champion Hustler Tournament, broadcast from Jansco's Showbar & Grill, where pool sharks gathered from all over America. It was the dead of winter, and I was operating the overhead camera from a hole cut in the attic floor. And I nearly froze to death.

Lord, You wouldn't send us to Chicago . . . would you?

But as days dragged by, I found myself thinking with disturbing frequency about Owen Carr and his crazy Chicago project. And though I tried to dig my heels in and keep out any thoughts about Chicago, my curiosity kept nagging me. Finally, I called Owen and arranged to meet with him.

On the hundredth floor of the John Hancock Building, I looked over the vast urban mission field and tried not to be impressed. I reminded myself how tough a television town Chicago was—the third largest market in the entire nation. This small band of Christians would be eaten alive by the monster-sized media powers in this city. In fact, the newspapers had already sunk their journalistic teeth into the fragile project, with every intention of tearing it apart.

But Owen Carr was for real. I sensed his deep, solid faith. I saw him weep because of his burden for Chicago's lost multitudes. I could not help but think of my hero, Albert Schweitzer, abandoning logic, ignoring pragmatism, and replacing them with faith.

I was impressed, but not enough to move to Chicago.

"I can't take the job," I finally told Owen. "But I'll give the matter some thought. Maybe I can recommend someone to you."

Shirley met me at the Norfolk airport with a hug, a kiss, and a wary "Well, what do you think?"

"Not much," I replied. "How are the kids?"

I did not want to talk about Chicago. I did not even want to think about it. But now it was Shirley's turn.

Two nights later, in the darkness of our bedroom, I glanced at Shirley. She was staring at the ceiling. I said something lighthearted, but she did not respond to my remark.

Instead, she said, "Honey, we're going to Chicago."

My smile went sour. "No, I don't believe we are." Case closed.

Are We Having Fun Yet?

The next day I got busy proving to myself that I meant it. I launched a big construction project, adding a thousand square feet to our attic. Determined to enjoy life on the East Coast, we broadened our horizons by visiting the nation's capital, historical Williamsburg—all the tourist traps in Newport News.

We are having fun, I told myself. *Life is great.*

But life was rotten.

I had a burr under my saddle. I was restless and unhappy at work. Although I was determined to stay with CBN, problems kept erupting. And for the first time in our marriage, Shirley and I could not enjoy our home.

"What's wrong with me?" I asked Shirley. "This is a perfect house for us. We're close to the bay. We've got plenty of room. But I feel so . . . unsettled."

"Me too," Shirley admitted. "Jerry, do you think God is trying to tell us something?"

"No," I moaned. "Not Chicago."

Chicago. Chicago. I could not stop thinking about the view I had seen of that city from the Hancock Building. Miles of streets, buildings, expressways lined with ritzy hotels, grim ghettos.

And then there was Owen Carr, the indomitable man with the invincible faith, driven by a vision to accomplish the impossible—a contemporary David taking on a giant task. Three months had passed since I had met with him. Maybe I should call him? Just out of courtesy?

"Look, I'm sorry," I stuttered on the phone. "I haven't been able to think of anyone for your project. Has . . . uh, has the job been filled?"

I was hoping against hope that it had been.

"No, it hasn't."

"Oh, well, just checking." We chatted briefly, then I hung up.

Within minutes, Owen called back. "Did you ask about the position's being filled because you're interested in filling it?"

"I don't really know," I hedged. "I guess I'm more interested than I was."

"Good!" he laughed. "I'm not surprised. I've been praying that the Lord would send you to us. I've asked God to give you the kind of passion for reaching the lost of Chicago that He's given me. We were just waiting for you, Jerry!"

I picked up right away on his use of the *past tense*. Suddenly, I felt like a fish who had been nibbling the bait. Now the hook was set.

But I was not ready to give up—not yet. "I'm not committing myself here, Owen," I protested. "But maybe Shirley and I should fly up and talk with you. I can't make a decision without her."

Owen agreed.

When we arrived in Chicago, the leaves had already fallen off the trees. As we left the airport, we stopped at a service station to use the phone. I asked the attendant for change.

"What do you think I am?" he snarled. "A bank? I don't have time to be giving change to every Joe that drops by."

Angered and embarrassed, I stalked back to the car. "Not exactly Mr. Southern Hospitality," I reported, slamming the car door.

"Jerry, would God do this to us?" Shirley asked.

"I don't know. Maybe."

We drove up and down the Chicago streets, past bums and mounds of garbage, past dozens of broken windows in cramped, bedraggled buildings. We craned our necks to see the tops of the skyscrapers and squinted in the glare of neon lights. We flinched at the clash of street noises and wrinkled our noses at unfamiliar city smells.

Chicago teemed with more people than we had ever imagined reaching with the gospel. We could not understand how God could possibly select us for this work, but we had the unmistakable feeling that God was etching Owen Carr's mission into our hearts and minds. If ever there was a time to know God's voice, this was it.

Sorting Through the Voices

I heard plenty of conflicting voices when I returned home from Chicago. My friends and colleagues in television ministry were horrified. They were sure that TV-38 would never survive, at least not as an all-

Christian station in a tough, crowded television town like Chicago. Signing on with them would be like setting sail on a sinking ship.

Neither Shirley nor I was fond of the idea of leaving comfortable Virginia where we could sail on the ocean every week and enjoy an endless array of fascinating historical outings. Chicago was Babylon—evil and foreign and far away.

My logic said no. The risks were enormous. *If the station fails, you fail*, I said to myself. *You've got to think of your career, your family.* Logic told me to safeguard my reputation in the television industry and stay away from TV–38. More than anything else in the world, I did not want to be known as a failure. Besides, I had been offered an opportunity to return to commercial television as manager for a CBS affiliate. The job promised good money in a nice town where my family could settle.

But through all the static, one voice said, "Go!"

It was God's voice.

"I Must Have an Answer!"

I was in the prayer room at CBN. The people in Chicago needed an answer from me, and I had committed to give them one that day. My back was to the wall as I cried out to God: *Lord, I must have an answer today!*

It made no sense for me to pack up and move my family to Chicago. Yet wasn't this one positive voice the same voice I had heard years before, saying, "I have a ministry for you"?

I sorted through the conflicting messages again; then

turned to that same source that I had turned to so often through the years—the one place where I was sure to hear God's voice—His Word.

I turned to Genesis 22:2 and read God's words to Abraham: "Take now your son, your only son Isaac, whom you love, and go to the land of Moriah, and offer him there as a burnt offering on one of the mountains of which I shall tell you."

Abraham could have argued, "But Lord, that doesn't make sense. Isaac is the only son I have. You gave him to me." But Abraham knew God's voice. He trusted that voice, and he obeyed it. God's blessing, as a result, was incalculable—an entire nation.

TV–38's beginnings had already defied logic. Owen Carr, essentially a rural preacher, had heard God's voice and obeyed. A man with no television experience was pursuing this dream. A handful of underfinanced businessmen had gathered to buy a powerful television station in a place like Chicago and were going to start a fully Christian station without generating income by selling commercials to sponsors.

And now God was asking me to suspend conventional wisdom and *join them*, to risk the one thing that I feared the most—the possibility of failing.

Was I willing to lay *my* Isaac—my career, my family, my home—on the altar? I turned to Isaiah 60:19 (TLB). The words pierced my heart: "No longer will you need the sun or moon to give you light, for the Lord your God will be your everlasting light, and he will be your glory."

In a flash of inspiration, the Lord showed me that I would be risking failure. All of my experience, my knowledge, my abilities were not enough for this job. I was indeed inadequate. But He was not concerned about that because He wanted to be my light. He simply wanted me to hear His voice and obey it.

But God, I protested in prayer, *I don't know anyone in Chicago.*

Suddenly, verse 21 (TLB) jumped out at me: "All your people will be good. They will possess their land forever, for I will plant them there with my own hands; this will bring me glory."

But God, the station hardly has any staff or supporters!

Verse 22 (TLB) answered my doubts: "The smallest family shall multiply into a clan; the tiny group shall be a mighty nation. I, the Lord, will bring it all to pass when it is time."

I could not resist His voice. I knew the call was real. *I want you to go,* the Lord was saying to me. *Invest all your energy, your ability, all the gifts I've given you. But these won't be enough. I will make up the difference.*

"We'll come to Chicago," I finally told Owen over the phone.

"Hallelujah!" he cheered.

"But there is one condition," I added. "I don't think I should be president. You have the vision; you fill the role of president. I'll come in as vice president and general manager."

"We'll work that out later," Owen said.

Deadly Inertia

I confess, now that I had obeyed, I was reluctant to go. I started thinking of ways to stall the actual move to

Chicago, perhaps until after Owen and his board had raised the money, bought the station, and secured the license. Then I would feel safer.

But I could sense the Lord cutting off my plan before it was formed.

Perhaps, I thought, *I can go to Chicago alone and leave Shirley and the children behind in case things don't work out, just until the station is on the air.*

Shirley shot that one down in an instant.

All too soon, we were packed and headed for the big city. It was an outlandish step of faith, more terrifying than rafting the Guadalupe. But the move was God's river; we knew we were headed for His destination. I had heard God's voice, and He said, "Go." The rest was up to Him.

The station struggled mightily during those early months and years. There were moments when it seemed the entire thing would collapse in a heap. Our working there required faith with a capital *F!* Frequently, I had to relive that moment in the CBN prayer room when I heard from God. That experience was my anchor. I often felt inadequate for the responsibility, but God kept His word to me and made up for everything I lacked.

Everybody Does It

Years later, after Owen had left TV–38 and the board had elected me president of the station, I was forced to submit to the river of God's will in one of the most difficult situations of my entire life.

The ministry had grown rapidly; we had a staff of eighty-five. With the rapid expansion, we had accumulated a debt of more than half a million dollars. I wanted to operate in the realm of faith—I wanted TV–38 to move forward, never back. But the burden continued to press on me.

Finally, one day, I fell back on a basic principle of inspirational faith: Tune in to God; tune out conflicting voices. I set aside a full day to seek God, tune in to His wavelength, and find out what He had to say about TV–38's financial situation.

As I prayed, God reminded me that faith meant obedience, and if that meant cutting back on our spending, then so be it. So I prayed, "Lord, we need a million dollars in this upcoming telethon, I'll understand that we are doing Your will in our finances. If we don't get the money, I'll cut the budget and work with what You give us."

I told the department managers about my decision. Either way, I wanted to be prepared, so for the next several days, we pored over budgets. On paper, we found fifty-thousand dollars per month that could be trimmed if absolutely necessary. The catch—these cuts would mean laying off twenty-two people. It was the only way.

The telethon came as scheduled—a beautiful, inspirational event, bringing in thousands of calls from viewers. We offered wonderful music from top performers and exciting, motivational messages from great preachers. But when the telethon ended, we were four-hundred thousand dollars short of our goal.

Some people urged me to press ahead, to maintain the *status quo*. They said that a cutback would signal a lack of faith. But I could not escape what God had laid at my feet on that long day when I fervently sought His will for the station.

I could have rationalized and continued to operate TV–38 in the red. We could have even shut down the ministry, I suppose. But that was not the course we chose, because that was not what God had called us to do. Instead, we submitted to the river of God's will.

On Monday morning we laid off twenty-two people. I never faced a tougher decision. I did not like God's will in this situation, but I cannot say I was surprised by it. We could lighten up in areas, cut some programs. We had gotten fat, and God had just put us on a crash diet.

I took the heat that day. People were angry and were accusing me of being cold and cruel. It hurt, but I knew what had to be done. And I knew it was God's will to do it.

The choice turned out to be a wise one. The river led us to our destination. God rewarded the ministry greatly. Within eight weeks we were operating in the black. The debt was eliminated. We had learned our lesson—at least for the time being!

Crossing the Street

God can also call us to do things we desperately *want* to do, and sometimes it is difficult to tune in to His voice simply because we are afraid that our longings may be garbling the message.

After operating out of the old ABC studios atop the Civic Opera Building on Wacker Drive, our ministry was squeezed to the limit. We urgently needed more space. Across the street stood the superb, state-of-the-art facilities of the Catholic Television Network, which were suddenly available at a price representing only a fraction of their value. But that simple move—just across the street—would require a 30 percent increase in our ministry's income.

I looked at our history, and I had my doubts. We had seen healthy annual increases—5 percent, 6 percent, 7 percent—but never anything approaching 30. The move would require three hundred thousand dollars a year more than we had ever brought in.

On our own it would have been impossible.

The risk was incredible. Financially, we had nothing to fall back on. We could lose the ministry. And I realized that my own reputation was at stake. If we moved and succeeded, people would call me a great man of faith; but if we moved and failed, I would be labeled a poor manager. My old fear of failure seemed to rear its ugly head within me again.

My mind was running in circles, but again, I tried to put a check on my thoughts and focus on God's voice. The important question was not whether we could make the move, but *did God want us to make the move?* When that question was settled, the rest of the questions would become unimportant. We would submit to God's will, we would walk in obedience, and we would leave the success or the failure of the venture to Him.

The ministry's management team was enthusiastic. One pointed out that the ministry could finally grow in bigger, better-equipped facilities. Another noted that the move would give the cramped, hard-working staff a much needed boost in morale.

"Don't kid yourself," I interrupted. "A new facility would only bring a short-term solution to your morale problem." Morale is more a spiritual problem than a physical one, I observed. Solve the spiritual problem, and the morale problem is solved as well. "Moving will mean a real faith struggle," I added, "and at the first sign of a problem in the new facility, that new morale will collapse. The grumblers will start to grumble again."

We needed more than morale as a reason to move. We needed to hear from God; we needed Him to sort out our desires of the flesh from His *best* for us. Just like you and I so often need to hear the voice of the Lord in our private lives, the leadership of TV–38 needed that crucial flash of inspirational faith. Hearing God's voice gives a tremendous surge of encouragement and energy. It can propel you forward to face the unknown for the cause of Christ. And your courage will challenge others to follow. When you are enflamed with the authority of God's calling, that authority rallies others to the cause.

Inspirational faith is essential to the Christian life, because it *moves* the church of Jesus Christ! Yet the fervor of inspirational faith can fade in the heat of the battle. That was the danger of letting our ministry take on this major financial challenge without our first hearing God's voice. When that fading time came, we needed to be able to remember the inspiration. We needed to have an actual moment of calling from the Lord that we could look back to, and hang on to as we pressed forward.

I presented the situation to the ministry's board of directors. "If this was just a business decision," one of them asked, "what would you do?"

"That's simple," I responded. "I wouldn't do it. It doesn't make a lot of business sense. Besides, why would I want to put myself at that much risk? The easiest thing for me to do is to back off. I'm safer staying here; my job is safer. But that's not the issue. The issue is this: What does God want us to do? That's what we have to know."

Then I asked them for the only thing they could really give—prayer.

"Gentlemen, I want us all to kneel and pray," I said. "I want us to seek God and keep on seeking Him until we have an answer, an answer we know beyond a shadow of a doubt is from God."

So we did. We knelt at our chairs, right there in the conference room and cried out to God, asking for divine direction—asking for a clear, distinct answer.

As I prayed, I thought about one of my favorite passages of Scripture, 1 Kings 18, in which the godly prophet Elijah challenges the pagan prophets of Baal to pray for a sign from heaven. Elijah, uniquely able to tune in to the voice of God, won that dramatic confrontation.

Elijah's situation was much like the one we faced at TV–38. It made no sense for him to lay down such a challenge, which was an affront to the heathen king. He was endangering his life. And who in his right mind would dare to boast that his God could send fire from heaven? Elijah, however, was operating on faith, not logic. He could put everything on the line because he recognized that voice. It was the same voice Owen Carr heard when he was inspired to launch TV–38; the same voice I had heard decades earlier, as a young boy standing at the kitchen sink; the same voice that launches the great missions of our day—the voice that cuts through the struggle between success and failure. It was the voice of God, and it demanded only one thing: obedience.

Fire streamed down from heaven, and Elijah won a stunning victory. Owen Carr saw his vision turn to reality as TV–38 broke over the airwaves on Memorial Day in 1976. And I had seen God make good on His calling to me so many years earlier.

Those who wait on the LORD shall renew their strength. As I prayed, Isaiah 40:31 pulsed through my spirit: *"They shall mount up with wings like eagles, they shall run and not be weary, they shall walk and not faint."*

On our knees, in that conference room, we prayed fervently for twenty minutes, then thirty, then forty. An hour passed, and we kept praying. Waiting for the Lord, just as Isaiah said.

Then, one by one, the members of the board got up. One by one, they expressed the calling: "I think God is saying yes." One more time, they were willing to hear from God and act on what He said. When they had all cast their votes, I told them, "I, too, believe God wants us to move. I don't understand it, but we'll do it."

It was an enormous step of faith for me. Noah must have felt something like I did as he received instructions for the ark. There was nothing left for me to do but start hammering!

Today it almost seems strange that we ever questioned the move. God gave us exactly the increase in income that we needed—a miracle boost of 30 percent that year. Our new home brought growth to our ministry and increased our effectiveness in touching the urban mission field for Christ. And we all experienced the truth, the thrill, of *genuine inspirational faith*—exactly the same faith that you can experience every single day of your life!

10

WORDS YOU DON'T WANT TO HEAR

God will speak words you don't want to hear, when He calls you to get involved in the lives of others. Not long ago a couple called and asked me to pray for their two-year-old daughter, who was in the hospital with cancer.

"We really do need your prayers," they said.

"Well, you have them," I replied. "I'll certainly be in prayer for you."

I hung up, but it was not over. The Lord began to speak to me.

That's not enough. This time I want you to be the answer to your own prayer.

I admit that I hesitated. I rationalized: I didn't know these people very well; I was busy. They were not my responsibility. But finally, I had to call them back.

"Go out to dinner," I said. "I really believe the Lord is telling me that I should sit up with your daughter while you go out and relax for a while."

"Oh, you don't have to do that," they protested.

"I know I don't, but I want to do this because the Lord is telling me to. I know you've had a heavy load, and I'd like to come sit with your daughter."

The story does not have the classic happy ending. The little girl died later. But in each word the Lord gives you, there is either something valuable for you or for someone else. In this case, God's word to me brought help and a brief moment of relief for a weary mom and dad. And I learned that I could not "hide" on television. I had to touch people personally as well as on the air. I had to go beyond the fear. In that simple experience of inspirational faith, God brought home to me the value of caring for His people, reminding me that sometimes He calls us not to an *action* but to an *attitude*.

I began to learn the value of genuinely caring for people in another ordinary but profound encounter with inspirational faith. When I was a young man, I worked as a disk jockey for KMAP-FM in Dallas. I was still single, so the crazy hours and madcap workload suited me perfectly. I worked every shift possible, filled in for every absence, learned everything I could about radio. Eventually, I was able to host a mellow late-night sign-off show called "Lovers and Losers," which featured slow, easy jazz—perfect for putting people to sleep.

One night as I was about to conclude the program, I opened the mike and spoke softly to my audience.

"Okay, you nightowls. It's time to go to bed. You just kick back now and relax while I put you to sleep with some easy-listening music."

Then, feeling laid back in the deep quiet of the night, I began wandering about with my words.

"Say, why don't you set your alarm about five minutes later than usual?" I suggested quietly, warmly. I pictured a listener—a female, living alone. "Give yourself some extra time to sleep in."

I went on in a rambling, lazy, sleepy voice.

"And hey, by the way, have you checked the door? You know better than to go to bed and leave your door unlocked. Check it out . . . That's right."

Like a friendly, intimate soulmate, I added, "Now just snuggle under those covers while I play you some gentle jazz."

Then I punched in the song—and the switchboard lit up in a blaze. Calls came from women all over Dallas. I got invitations to breakfast, lunch, and otherwise. It was as if I had broken some emotional dam. Many called to tell me their problems. You would have thought I was a psychologist.

At first I was dumbfounded, but soon I realized what had happened. Lonely women of all ages and backgrounds needed someone to care about them. The sound of my voice, the concern I expressed for their safety and comfort, appealed to them. My caring—even if it came out of an electronic box—came as a rare and unique gift to brighten their sad, empty lives. They called because they thought maybe, just maybe, the man on the radio really was concerned about their loneliness, their hurt, their insecurities. That experience laid the foundation for the counseling ministry that is so vital to TV-38.

I could not help but think of my own childhood—the heartbreaking moments when I thought no one cared about me or appreciated me. I remembered how I clung to any expression of friendship. I recalled the deep isolation of feeling inadequate and useless. Of course, I had dealt with most of my hurts years before, but these people, crying out to a radio disk jockey, had never escaped their torment. They had never found anyone or anything to pull them out of their despair.

A Channel of Help

As I signed off the air that night, the experience hung in my mind like a heavy mist that would not evaporate. Three distinct impressions came out of the mist.

First, I saw people's desperate need for someone to care about them.

Second, I was jolted by the power I seemed to have over these women because of my position in the media. If I had not really cared—if I had been irresponsible and calloused—I could have accepted some of their offers, exploited them, and abused their trust. I had seen plenty of radio and television personalities do just that.

And third, I realized that the first two impressions dovetailed in a powerful way. The power of the media could be used to *help* meet these people's needs. With its power to reach across the land or even overseas, a television or radio station could broadcast a message of hope, love, and forgiveness to the hurting, the lonely, the isolated. And people could receive that help without fear of exploitation or abuse. They could call in to the station and find a loving, dedicated, godly man or woman to listen to them and guide them out of their despair, into the hope of faith, by way of God's practical Word.

That stunning, intensely personal moment of inspirational faith reshaped my attitudes and perspectives toward the media and toward ministry for the rest of my life. But it was only a few months later when God tested me on what I had learned.

WORDS YOU DON'T WANT TO HEAR

During one of my late-night broadcasts, the phone rang. Marsha, a tough, bitter salesperson, whom I had previously met, was calling.

"What're ya' doin'?" she asked. Her slurred speech suggested she had been drinking.

"My show," I answered matter-of-factly. "What are *you* doing?"

"I'm at a party . . . havin' a good time."

Before I could even make a casual response, she interrupted.

"No, that's not right. I'm havin' a miserable time. I need to talk to somebody. Could I talk to you?"

I hesitated. I wanted to help but instinctively wanted to avoid getting involved. Somewhere in her voice, though, I detected a note of sincerity.

"I'm leaving this party," Marsha muttered. "It's terrible. Can I come to the radio station and talk to you?"

Although I didn't fear the circumstance's being improper, I was still reluctant to let her come. "I guess that would be O.K.," I stammered. "I finish at one."

She was waiting for me in her car at quitting time. As I sat in the passenger seat of her car, I was overwhelmed by the reek of cheap perfume, cigarette smoke, and alcohol. A vivid picture of my father flashed through my mind, and I rolled down the window.

"Nice Guy"

Marsha was unpleasant to look at. Her hair was a big fluff of orange cotton candy; she wore a tasteless red dress and matching heels. And her heavy makeup gave her eyes a skeletal look.

"Thanks for seeing me," Marsha said, then took a long drag on her cigarette and blew the smoke at the windshield. "You seem like a nice guy, Jerry. . . ." She crushed the cigarette butt in an overflowing ashtray. Then, with a grim nonchalance, she asked the question I was afraid she might ask. Obviously, she thought it was expected of her.

"No," I responded evenly. "That's not why I'm here."

Marsha looked relieved. "Good. I really meant it when I said I just needed someone to talk to."

Then, without another moment's hesitation, she began to pour out her story. Marsha was struggling to raise her three children alone and dealing with intense feelings of rejection as a result of a painful divorce. As she talked, her demeanor softened from her usual tough, sarcastic self to a frightened, vulnerable child. After a long while, she stopped to dab at the streaks of mascara on her cheeks and asked if we could get something to eat.

I hesitated—again. The only place open at that hour was a restaurant near the airport—one of the busiest restaurants in the city. I was horrified to think of being seen with her there. It was one thing to sit in a dark parking lot with this woman, but it was another thing entirely to walk in under the bright glare of the restaurant's fluorescents with her. I could easily imagine one of the deacons from my church, sitting at the counter at the end of his late shift, choking on his hamburger as I walked in with this woman in red. What a choice bit of gossip I could manufacture.

My face flushed as I realized my selfishness. I

thought of the Samaritan woman at the well—an adulteress, a vile sinner, whom Jesus did not hesitate to be seen with. He responded not to her status but to her need. He was not concerned about what people thought of Him but only about how He could help her. And I realized that as a Christian, the best place for me to be was sitting in a restaurant booth with Marsha in the middle of the night.

I relaxed, and we headed for the restaurant. There, she kept talking; I kept listening. It was a sad encounter, not only because of Marsha's story but because I knew she represented millions of women—tough on the outside, hurt on the inside.

When she ended her story, I spoke up. "I think I know a way to help you." Then I told her about Jesus and His love for her.

"I don't know about all that religious stuff," she shrugged. "Maybe I'll think about it. If you recommend Him, He can't be all bad."

And that was that.

I am not sure what happened to Marsha. I pray she took my advice, but I'll probably never know. What I do know is that God used that experience to teach *me*, to deeply impress me not only with the need of the lost but with the importance of my—of all believers'— *responding* to that need rather than responding to the pressures to maintain my own reputation.

God designed people to need each other. God's will is that we help each other. God's plan is that we clearly hear Him when He calls us to minister to others, even those we deem unpleasant. So many of us accept Christ in a flush of emotion and enthusiasm but then live to keep that good feeling, maintain our emotional comfort level. God's design is not for us to spend every moment in the happy, carefree fellowship of the saints. God's design is for us to invade the world with His love, as He opens doors of opportunity to us and speaks His divine appointments to our hearts.

Do you hear His voice but avoid obedience? We all do, in some ways. We fear rejection, we're afraid of looking silly; we have our own agenda for life.

Ask yourself these hard questions, and see yourself as you really are.

- How often do I really not want to listen to God's voice?
- How often have I heard but not acted?
- How much do I worry about looking foolish if I do what God wants me to do?
- When was the last time I missed an opportunity to be God's instrument to help others?
- Am I too busy to listen to and obey God's voice?
- Am I close enough to Christ to hear His voice?

11

REMEMBER THE INSPIRATION

My daughter, Vanessa, now eleven years old, teaches me spiritual principles without realizing it. One spring she got excited about the idea of planting a garden. We put together a twelve-by-six-foot garden box, bought special soil, visited the nursery, and planted tomatoes and carrots and other vegetables. She was thrilled, enchanted by the whole process.

A month later, I found myself alone in the garden, pulling weeds, thinning carrots, watering, fertilizing, nurturing the soil. Vanessa was nowhere to be seen. She had, of course, lost the passion. Her inspiration had withered, and the now boring circumstances had deflated her enthusiasm.

In the Christian walk, you can expect similar experiences, and you can counteract them when you remember the inspiration. Remember God's word to you and then continue to walk in that word. In my first six traumatic months with the television station in Chicago, I had to review *every single day* my calling, just to keep from fleeing. Even now, more than a decade later, I still have to review that calling from time to time to keep the memory fresh, to keep myself on course. I have to keep remembering I am here because God called me here. *God's will does not change with the circumstances.* You cannot run, as Jonah learned en route to Tarshish. Even when it is old, God's calling is still true; you must keep it alive in your life until you know God has called you to do something different.

When you remember your calling you will stay in the flow of God's will for your life. I had to learn this lesson the hard way shortly after I lost the job opportunity with the Southern Baptists. I was still stewing over the turn of events, still "pacing in my cell," anxious to get into Christian communications, when I was recommended for the operations director position at Doubleday Broadcasting's El Paso station. I certainly did not want the job; it was secular work again, and I had had more than nine years of that by now. I figured it was about time for God to move me into Christian work, and that seemed more likely to happen if I stayed in a big city like Dallas.

But Shirley, as usual with much keener insight, asked me a perceptive question: "Is there any area of the television industry where you still need some experience?"

Yes, there was one such area—management.

"And what kind of position are they offering you in El Paso?" she asked sweetly.

I cleared my throat and mumbled, "Management."

"Then," she added, "this could be God, couldn't it?"

"Could be," I had to admit.

"You're the Couple"

The following weekend, we were on a plane to El Paso, scheduled for interviews at the station. But I still did not have a clear picture on this. *Was El Paso God's will for me right now?*

I was still praying about it as we flew home. The job was mine for the taking, but I urgently wanted some firm assurance from the Lord before I made such a move.

Suddenly, I saw a familiar face: There on the plane was the pastor of a church in El Paso we had attended that weekend. As he was coming down the aisle, I stopped him and introduced myself.

"Oh, *you're* the couple," he said. I was surprised that he recognized our names.

"We are?" I asked. He sat down in the seat beside us. "You know, the general manager of the station was at our church on Sunday."

I hadn't known that; the man wasn't even a Christian.

"He came down to the altar at the end of the service," the pastor continued, "and said, ' I want you to pray for me because I'm interviewing a guy today. He could become the operations manager at the television station. I really would like to have the influence of a Christian at our station.' "

I could almost feel the Lord nudge me, saying, "There's your answer."

From that moment, even before the corporate headquarters had cleared the offer officially, I knew we were going. I knew it was God's will. God's timing. God's everything.

Without any real surprises, I got the job; we agreed on a salary, and we moved everything we owned to El Paso. On my second day at the station, the manager called me into his office. It was time for a surprise.

"I have some bad news," he said, embarrassed. "I can't give you the salary we agreed on."

I felt my neck get hot, but I remained soft-spoken while being straightforward with him. "Either pay me or I'm leaving."

He shifted uncomfortably in his chair. "I'm sorry, but we really have a problem."

"No, we don't have a problem," I retorted. "*You* have a problem. You're going to have to deal with it. This is what you promised me, and that's what I expect, or I'm leaving."

"I don't know quite what to do," he protested.

"Sorry," I replied. "I know what you need to do. You need to get in touch with the corporate office and tell them what's going on. I simply expect what you promised—nothing more and nothing less."

Whose Problem Is This?

I thought I had handled the situation pretty well, but before I got home that evening, the Lord was taking me to task. *Did I call you to this job or not?* He demanded. I had only two options: either validate my calling or deny my calling. Either God had called me there, or He hadn't—nothing complicated. The answer, of course, was that God had called me there. He was in charge, not me.

And you're going to let salary stand in your way? I felt God's persistent touch. All my glib arrogance melted. With tears in my eyes, I explained the episode to Shirley. She agreed; God first.

The next morning I swallowed my pride and apologized to the station manager: "I'm sorry. I'll take whatever you pay. This is where I belong, and I'm going to stay. Whatever you decide will be fine."

The end of the story had a happy twist. The station gave me a car and a travel allowance and provided brand-new drapes for our new house. As grateful as I was for these extras, they didn't really matter. What mattered was that I had learned to do what God *said* to do—I had remembered my calling. In the tough times remember your calling. It becomes an anchor that keeps you from drifting.

Years later I was in a position to pass this teaching along to an employee I had hired at TV–38. He testified in his home church that the Lord had really "opened this door" to him, but he found it rough going. Before long he came to me and informed me that he intended to quit.

"Didn't you stand up in church and say this was God's will for your life?" I demanded quietly.

He admitted he had.

"Then one of two things is true," I said. "Either you're walking away from God's will, or it wasn't God's will in the first place."

This young man missed an opportunity to allow God to develop spiritual character. He left bitter, and later he walked away from God. He never learned. Sadly, I have seen many others make the same mistake: They use "It wasn't God's will" as a cop-out when life grows too uncomfortable for their tastes.

Inspirational faith is not a flash in the pan. It keeps inspiring you to fulfill God's best for you, even when situations go awry. In his book, *The Pursuit of Holiness*, Jerry Bridges says, "The path of obedience is often contrary to human reason. If we do not have conviction in the necessity of obeying the revealed will of God as well as confidence in the promises of God, we will never persevere in this difficult pursuit."[1]

Feeling No Grief

Sometimes you must remember your calling simply for the sake of your own spiritual health. One day on my television program I welcomed a thoroughly unimpressive young man. He sported a punk hairdo, a too-long coat, and ridiculous baggy pants tied at the ankles. *Just what we need*, I thought to myself. *Another "designer missionary!"*

But this was Youth With A Mission's David Pierce, a missionary to Amsterdam. During the interview I asked him how he and his wife could work among the flagrant sin and deviant immorality of Amsterdam's red-light district without being affected spiritually. His answer was profound.

"We decided that if we ever walked down the street and didn't feel grief for the sin we saw, we'd leave the city for two weeks to fast and pray until that burden came back."

I was stunned, moved deeply by those words. This couple was serious about their calling, serious enough to make sure they never lost the zeal for the souls they had been called to reach. They were looking back to the day their hearts were broken by that ugly mission field. They were returning to their source of inspirational faith.

Christ's words in Matthew 13:19-22 (TLB), explaining His parable of the sower, cut to the heart of this crucial point:

> The shallow, rocky soil represents the heart of a man who hears the message and receives it with real joy, but he doesn't have much depth in his life, and the seeds don't root very deeply, and after a while, when trouble comes, or persecution begins because of his beliefs, his enthusiasm fades, and he drops out. The ground covered with thistles represents the man who hears the message, but the cares of this life and his longing for money choke out God's Word, and he does less and less for God.

What a sad portrait of the Christian life. Perhaps you see these words apply to you more than you would like. Happily, Jesus goes on in verse 23 to describe a worthier model for our lives today: "The good ground represents the heart of a man who listens to the message and understands it and goes out and brings thirty, sixty, or even a hundred others into the kingdom." That's what you can accomplish when you remember the inspiration and live it daily!

How Do You Hear?

God does not reserve His guidance just for career choices and other big decisions of life. He wants to lead you every day, talk to you about everyday subjects. Inspirational faith is essential to every aspect of your life. The problem is that you can become too busy to listen if you spend most of your time mapping out a forest when you need to be strolling among the trees.

Often as you read His Word, you will hear God speak silently in your spirit. Sometimes I almost audibly hear His voice; and I instinctively know that it is God's voice, just as I did that day, so long ago, standing at my mother's kitchen sink. At other times, God's voice comes to me like a blow to my midsection. Usually I feel this way when I've done something wrong, and it's time to confront the error. Sometimes God's voice is just a whisper or a nudge, as when the Holy Spirit urges me to call or visit or pray for someone.

Perhaps you have felt a sense of restraint in your spirit as you began a project or activity; the Lord was cautioning you not to be involved. Or you may have felt prompted to say a word to a friend without really knowing why. God can speak to you in countless different ways; but as you learn to know His voice, each new word will sound more and more familiar. No matter how you hear from God and no matter how large or small the task He sets before you, it is when you hear from God that you can accomplish things for the kingdom. God has a plan, and the closer you are to Him, the more you will be an effective part of it.

When we moved to Virginia Beach, Shirley and I bought a house that came with loads of furniture, including a side-by-side refrigerator and a washing machine. I immediately thought of staging a big garage sale. "We'll make some money off this stuff," I told Shirley. But before she could even answer, I felt God speaking otherwise to my heart: *I've given these to you. Don't sell them; give them away.*

My first thought was that a message about something as mundane as furniture and appliances could not have come from God, so I brushed the thought aside. But it would not stay gone, and I finally realized that the Lord really was telling me not to sell these things. I was actually to give them away. He had blessed us, and now He wanted us to be a blessing to others.

I put out the word at the office that I had some large appliances, and if anybody wanted them, they could let me know. Ben Kinchlow came forward. He had worked as discipleship director at the CBN station in Dallas when I had worked there and had come to Virginia Beach at about the same time I had. Of course, he went on to cohost *The 700 Club* and to become a well-known international ministry personality in his own right.

"Jerry, I hear you have a refrigerator for sale," he said. "How much do you want for it?"

"I can't sell it to you," I responded. "If you want it, I

have to give it to you. I really believe that's what God wants me to do."

Ben's eyes lit up. "You're not going to believe this," he said, "but when we left Dallas, our refrigerator died. I was going to load it on the truck, bring it with us, and have it repaired here, but I felt the Lord telling me to leave it. I said, 'But Lord, we don't have the money to buy another one when we get to Virginia. What are we going to do?' We finally decided to leave it, and now this happens. Praise God; He really does provide!"

CBN Music Director "Moose" Smith, who had moved up from North Carolina, approached me one afternoon. "I understand you have a washing machine," he said. "Could my wife and I take a look at it? We'd like to buy it."

After I convinced him I couldn't sell it, he brought his wife over to see it. When they walked into our garage, she began to weep. Moose just stood there with his mouth open.

"What's wrong?" I asked.

"You're not going to believe this," he began (exactly Ben's words). "When we left North Carolina, we rented a U-Haul truck. We loaded the thing up and didn't have room for our washer; so we had to sell it, but we didn't get near enough money to buy another one like it. My wife's been going to the laundromat. This washing machine is the same make, the same size, the same color as the one we left behind!"

So Ben and Moose and their families got their divinely appointed appliances. But far more importantly, we all learned more about the power and love of God and how we can trust Him to provide for us and for others through us. We learned the value of listening to His still, small voice, even in the mundane, everyday twists and turns of life!

One obstacle to inspirational faith, an obstacle to obeying God's voice that many of us carry within, usually without realizing it, is low self-esteem. If we possess a negative image of ourselves, we can fail to function at our full effectiveness and not fulfill God's plan for our lives. We hear from God, but we can't believe that we could accomplish anything for Him.

I know this territory because I've been there.

12

GARBAGE MAN

For many years before he became a Christian, my father looked to alcohol as an escape from his insecurities, inadequacies, and fears. Sadly, the alcohol set him on a downward spiral and instead of soothing him, increased his self-loathing.

Dad was not a blind drinker. He knew himself, and he was embarrassed by what he knew. Some days he would come home in a drunken stupor. He did crazy things. He broke lamps. He shouted into the street. Later, when he sobered up, he would apologize, humiliated. He felt bad about the trouble he had caused.

During these times, he wanted to make up to us for his behavior so badly that I could have asked for the moon and he would have tried to get it for me. His remorse told me he was not a monster; he was a man caught in the grip of his insecurities and Satan's lies. He had turned away from God and bought into the deceit of alcohol. Drinking became a mountain of trash in his life that seemed impossible to remove.

When Dad was drinking, I feared him and did my

best to stay clear of him. At school, my stomach would fill with dread as the dismissal bell rang. I knew when I got home, he would be there—maybe drunk, stumbling about, cursing, fuming, threatening. Sometimes I would go to a pay phone and call my mother to check on his condition. I could tell by the hesitation in her voice if he was drunk.

Ultimately, calling her was pointless. I still had to go home, despite Dad's condition. But on days when Mom hesitated, when I knew he was drunk, I walked more slowly. I hoped that my delay would give Dad time to be a little bit better, a little less mean, or passed out by the time I arrived.

As I grew older and bigger, I was sometimes able to turn my love into courage. More than once as a youngster of twelve, I stood in front of the door and declared to my drunken father, "If you leave this house, you'll have to go through me!" Through glazed eyes, he glared at me and threatened to beat me. Sometimes he pushed me aside. But he never hit me. Even then, his love for his family was at work, somewhere deep inside.

Such a childhood influenced me. I avoided alcohol like the plague, but without a strong fatherly role model, I gained little self-confidence and numerous insecurities. I moved toward adulthood heavy-laden with self-doubt. As a result, even the normal struggles of youth had a more damaging impact on me than they might have otherwise. My protruding teeth and five years of braces made me feel extremely self-conscious. In school I felt incompetent and untalented and had no ambition for personal accomplishment. Success was a foreign word. And, as I coped with my perceived worthlessness, I had to deal with the embarrassment my father caused me.

Actually, I was not embarrassed by his drinking. Lots of my friends' fathers drank. The real source of my humiliation was his *job*: My dad drove a garbage truck. Although sanitation work is good, steady employment, I didn't understand that then. My friends' fathers had more "noble" jobs. Freddy's father was an accountant, and their family had a nice house with all the amenities. My family always seemed to be poor.

Dad didn't have much of an education, and he had even less self-confidence. For nearly thirty-seven years he drove a route with two fellows who worked for him and rode shotgun on his truck. Whenever he came up for promotion to foreman, he declined. He just could not see himself as a manager.

As I absorbed his low self-esteem, I tried to mask my fears by breaking rules. Fortunately, my mother dragged me to church every Sunday, prayed for me fervently, and lived a godly life before me. Eventually, it paid off. But even after I had accepted Christ—even after I had recognized my rebellious behavior for the sham that it was and had put all that nonsense behind me—it still took years to work through the host of insecurities that I had harbored within for so long.

The Alice Fallacy

Pretty Alice Cranford—hands down the most beautiful girl in our school, if not in the entire world—still stands in my memory as a symbol of my struggle. I had a crush on her in the ninth grade. So did every other boy in the school.

Although I had lettered in football—an accomplishment that would have attracted most high-school girls—the idea of my going out with Alice Cranford never entered my mind—at least not as a real possibility. In fact, there wasn't a guy in my circle of friends who came close to qualifying for a date with such a girl. She was way out of our humble league.

But one day a friend of mine came walking down the school hallway, looking dazed, and reported breathlessly, "I've got a date with Alice."

"You're crazy!" I said. "It's impossible for anyone to get a date with Alice. Especially you!"

"No! It's true!" he replied, his eyes wide. "I asked her and she said yes."

My throat went dry. I couldn't believe it. My friend, my buddy, had a date with *the* Alice Cranford.

Then I had an astonishing thought: *Hey! If that guy can get a date with her, why couldn't I?*

That afternoon I ran home, picked up the telephone, and called Alice. She said yes.

Our date was a dream, like a scene from one of those romantic books—it was fantasy. We went to a school basketball game. We laughed and talked and cheered for our side. We had a wonderful evening.

But that night, long after I had taken her home and returned to the dark of my own quiet bedroom, my mind began to replay the scenes and rewrite them. Alice was only pretending to have fun. She couldn't possibly have had a good time with someone like me.

Me, of all people! She was probably going to tell everybody at school what a loser I was. Jerry Rose, the world's biggest loser. She would probably never go out with me again, and I certainly was not about to call her to find out.

I made good on that decision. I went through school, graduated, and left town without another date or meaningful conversation with Alice Cranford.

Twelve years later, Shirley and I were visiting one of my old school pals, Mike Lambeth, and his wife, Linda. Typically, our reunion turned into a memory-fest.

"Hey, do you remember Alice Cranford?" Linda asked me.

I laughed. "Are you kidding? Who could forget Alice?" And then, with an inkling of gloating, I added, "We had a date once."

"Yeah, I know," Linda smirked. "She thought you were the biggest snob in school."

"What? Me? Why?"

"Because after your date, she was crazy about you," Linda replied, grinning. "She had a crush on you for months. But you never asked her out again. You wouldn't even speak to her!"

While Shirley, Mike, and Linda laughed, I laid my head on the dining room table and moaned. I was overwhelmed by how wrong my thinking had been and how I can still struggle with life when I base decisions on *faulty perceptions of myself*.

How might *your* life be different if you had seen yourself differently at key points along the way? if you could see yourself with the potential God sees in you? Your value to the kingdom of God—your effectiveness as a member of the body of Christ—is related very closely to the view you hold of yourself. My psychologist friend, Dr. Vern McNally, calls this "the story we tell ourselves about ourselves." When you tell yourself a story of incompetence, inability, and hopelessness, you produce accordingly. But as a Christian, you should be telling yourself the story that God has written about you—the story of the King's child, fit for service, equipped supernaturally to do the work of the Master. I decided a long time ago that if God told me to do something, I could do it, regardless of what I thought.

The Vanessa Lesson

I can now look back at my childhood and recall good times, healthy times, times when I was not embarrassed but, in fact, was proud of my dad. He had wonderful qualities as well as terrible flaws, but in those days I only *observed* his strengths, while I saw and took on his weaknesses.

I sometimes rode his route with him. I was thrilled to sit in the cab of that massive truck and watch my father in action. Somehow the two men who worked with my dad never looked as clean and sharp as he did. His hair was always neatly combed, and his khaki pants and white shirt were always starched and pressed. The others clearly respected him.

The people on his route knew him by name and enjoyed it when he stopped to talk. He was welcomed as a favored visitor in the restaurants along the route. The owner of the grill often gave us a free breakfast while he chatted with Dad. Later in the day we would stop at Sammy's Restaurant, where Sammy always had a piece of pie for "Rose's kid" and a whole pie to take home to the family. At the barbecue place, Dad and I would be greeted with a warm welcome and a sack of barbecue sandwiches to take home to Mom and Judy.

Dad did his job well and established warm relationships along the way. In fact, he was on such good terms with the head of sanitation for the entire city of Dallas that he was able to secure me an excellent summer job in the Sanitation Department three years in a row. As I sat in the Sanitation office, far from the tedious, menial labor most of my fellow high schoolers were enduring, it finally began to dawn on me just how special my father really was.

When I was introduced, people would nod and smile and say, "Oh, you're Rose's kid." And when Dad visited me in the office, I could see that the city employees regarded him as more than "just a garbage man": He was a valued fellow laborer in the work of the municipality. Dad was teaching me, without my knowing it, traits like perseverance, dignity, consistency—traits I have grown to respect and treasure.

Now that I am a father myself and have grown spiritually through the years, I tell myself a different story about my childhood and about me. I see others differently, with more compassion. And sometimes I have to edit and rewrite my children's view of themselves and others.

When Vanessa was in the third grade, Shirley and I received some distressing news from her school. Vanessa and several other children had been teasing and taunting a little girl because of her father's vocation: He was a garbage man.

I immediately called the little girl's mother, apologized for my daughter's misbehavior, and assured her that I would take action to correct it. But then I told her that my father had had the same occupation as her husband, and I described his positive example to me as I grew into adulthood. Although I never met that little girl's mother, I felt close to her in this sharing.

That afternoon I sat one nervous third-grader on my lap and asked her to tell me about the trouble at school. She related her side of the story; then it was my turn.

"Do you know what Grandpa Rose did when I was in third grade like you and he was a dad like me?"

Vanessa fidgeted anxiously. This was a curve ball. She loved her granddad. He could do no wrong. "No," she responded uneasily. "What?"

"He was a garbage man."

Vanessa straightened up; her dark eyes widened. "Really?" she squealed. Well, then, she decided, being a garbage man must be a good thing. She returned to school, went to the wronged little girl, and offered a big—and I believe heartfelt—apology.

13

REWRITING THE STORY

You may find it difficult to rewrite the story you tell yourself. Others may be repeating the negative story. Once again, you have to screen out the static and tune in to the voice of the Lord. You must learn to hear God by continuing to practice inspirational faith.

One of my high-school teachers in my hometown of Pleasant Grove filled my mind with static. Mr. Horstrom intimidated me fiercely—not physically, but mentally.

"Rose," he growled, "you're never going to amount to anything. You'll end up with some local girl, take a local job, and spend the rest of your life in the Grove. A local yokel—that's what you'll end up being."

There is nothing wrong with spending your life in your hometown with your childhood sweetheart and a good, steady job. But Horstrom was indicting me by implication, suggesting I could never achieve or excel. His accusation sounded horrible, and the words stuck. I'll never forget that verdict pronounced on me.

Years later, when I had come a long way toward learning to hear God and trusting His leading, I flew to Europe for the first time. I was going to assist a group in France who were interested in developing a Christian television program. As I flew over England, I pulled out my diary and made an entry: "Today I beat Horstrom. My wife is not a local, my career is not local, and I have just become international. By the grace of God, Horstrom is defeated. I am not a 'local yokel.' "

It was no credit to me that the spectre of Horstrom's prophecy was no longer hanging over me. It was testimony to God's patience and grace in my life. Long years after I had accepted Christ, after I had accepted His call to the ministry, even after I had worked in full-time Christian service for several years, I finally began to understand the story that God had written about me, and how it differed from my story and Horstrom's story. I still don't fully understand it, but I am further down the road than I was the day Horstrom sneered in my face. Today, I can see by my own experience that even when I cannot do a job, if God calls me to it, He will accomplish His purpose through me.

I have seen this principle at work countless times. When I went to a CBS station as operations manager, for example, I had no experience in operations. But God clearly signaled me to take the position, even though it was at a secular station. By that point in my Christian walk, I was able to tell myself a more confident story about me: not "I can do it" but "God knows something I don't—He can do it through me."

Several years ago, Shirley and I were fortunate enough to visit Italy. We toured the museums and the galleries; we marveled at the masterpieces. I was deeply moved by Michaelangelo's sculptures, the *Pieta* and the *David*. Michaelangelo's work was so perfect that he deliberately flawed one of the knees of his *Moses* because he believed that mere man had no right to create something so lifelike. It was stunning to realize that these fabulous, detailed works of art were cut from something as ordinary as a *rock*.

The heart of Michaelangelo's genius was that he could look at a plain rock and *see* a beautiful sculpture. He had a vision of the finished product. From the first blow of the hammer on the chisel, he knew what the *Pieta* would look like. He saw Mary in her sorrow, holding her dead son in her arms. Before the first chip of rock fell away, Michaelangelo could envision David's rippling muscles and expressive face. The sculptor simply cut away everything that was not part of that vision.

Likewise, God saw in Gideon not what Gideon was but what he could become. God saw in David not what David was but what he could become. The Master Sculptor sees not what you are but what He can make of you if you allow Him to chip away everything that is not part of His vision for you. God can carve masterpieces out of our rocklike wills. If you give Him a free hand, He can transform you into an exquisite creation!

My friend James Payne wrote a song that beautifully captures this truth:

> *Cut from the rock by the Sculptor's hand*
> *Made in His image, according to His plan.*
> *That's why I don't worry when troubles come my*
> *way.*
> *I'm trusting in the word of God, and I'm cut from*
> *the rock.*[1]

God's sculpting of you is a daily process, a lifelong process. And it can be an uncomfortable process. I have been a Christian most of my life, and the chips are still flying. But the promise I claim for myself—and the promise I claim on your behalf—is the promise of Philippians 1:6 (TLB): "I am sure that God who began the good work within you will keep right on helping you grow in his grace until his task . . . is finally finished on that day when Jesus Christ returns."

You must hear from God and submit to His voice. Then you can become everything God has in mind for you to become and accomplish everything God has in mind for you to accomplish!

The Fugitive

David, perhaps more than any other character in the entire Scripture record, had reason to wallow in low self-esteem and excuse himself from accomplishing anything for God. He was a small, seemingly insignificant lad, the youngest of seven brothers, constantly slighted and humiliated by the older boys. When the prophet Samuel came to the house to anoint one of Jesse's sons as the next king, Jesse did not even bother to call little David in from the pasture where he was serving in the lowly capacity of shepherd. Jesse did not believe God would be interested in the boy. Like Mr. Horstrom, he had already written a negative, short-sighted story for the youngster.

God's calling did not guarantee David smooth-sailing. Nor does God's calling guarantee smooth-sailing for you and me today. After Samuel's amazing anointing service, David still had to face the mockery of his brothers, the vicious hypocrisy of King Saul, and years as a fugitive. If anyone should have felt inferior, it was David.

I do not believe it was easy for David to forget the hurts. I believe he struggled with self-confidence just as you and I do. But David poured out all his frustration and doubt to the Lord and remembered the calling. And years later, when he had opportunities to exact revenge on those who had wronged him, he embraced them instead because revenge was not part of his calling.

The Empty Chair

Self-esteem is crucial to inspirational faith. You must believe you can accomplish God's calling. But even the term *self-esteem* does not accurately describe the confidence you need. Your confidence is not in yourself but in God's calling. You need only be confident that you are doing your best to hear that calling and act on it. You cannot do it on your own. God will do it through you.

God needs you to hear His voice, to trust His calling, and to obey His leading. He has a plan for you that no one else can quite fulfill. Jonathan admonished his friend David in 1 Samuel 20:18 (TLB), "They will miss you tomorrow when your place at the table is empty." These words apply to you today because God has a place at His table for you—just as He has a place for me and a place for my wife, Shirley and a place for every member of the body of Christ. You have a calling; you have a task to accomplish that is not quite the same as mine. God needs *you*.

"God gives us many kinds of special abilities," Paul wrote in 1 Corinthians 12:4-7 (TLB). "There are different kinds of service to God . . . there are many ways in which God works in our lives, but it is the same God who does the work in and through all of us who are his. The Holy Spirit displays God's power through each of us as a means of helping the entire church." How does God want to work in your life? How does God want to display His power through you as a means of helping the entire Church?

The Prayer Gift

One night during a fund-raising telethon at TV–38, a woman, obviously in deep despair, called our studio.

"I really want to help," she sobbed, "but I have no money. All I can do is pray."

"Wait a minute," I interjected. "What do you mean, 'all you can do is pray'? That's one of the most beautiful and needed gifts you can give to this ministry!"

The woman calmed down. When she hung up, she realized that she was every bit as important to our ministry family as the biggest donor. God called her to give the gift of prayer. Somebody else was called to give money.

God will speak to you about your role. As you tune in

to His voice, His leading will become clear to you. As you long to hear Him, to obey Him, to fulfill His calling in your life, He will use you in beautiful and perhaps surprising ways.

God's will is not a mysterious phantom, intended to be difficult to grasp. God's will is His best and most effective plan for your life, from the biggest accomplishments to the tiniest details of your life. Remember the words of my pastor-friend: "God wants His will for you even more than you want it!"

Part 3
SURVIVAL FAITH

14

"I WILL NOT GIVE UP"

Annette came into my office, her eyes red and puffy from what I guessed had been a night of tears. In one hand she held a shredded Kleenex, in the other a well-worn Bible. She had been in before, sometimes alone, sometimes with her husband. Their marriage had been held together for years by the single thread of her faithfulness.

I hadn't seen Jim in a while. During his last counseling session, he had told me, "I don't feel like I have control over myself. I don't want to hurt Annette, but I love Jane. If I divorce Annette and marry Jane, God will forgive me, won't he?"

"Yes, Jim," I said, "He probably will. But you'll never forgive yourself. And I doubt the marriage will last. First of all, you won't trust each other. So don't look for happiness. In my opinion, you're headed for misery."

I knew, from the desperate look in Annette's eyes, that Jim had made his decision.

"Jim told me last night; he wants a divorce." Her words came out haltingly, as if she were letting them escape through the dam she had built to contain a flood of emotions and tears.

"Maybe it's time to give up then," I sighed, "and get on with your life."

"I can't do that," Annette insisted. "I love him. I'm not going to let Satan ruin what we had. I know what type of man he can be. That woman could destroy him."

This was not new ground. We had had similar conversations previously, but Annette always persisted in hanging on. The last time she had come in, I had confronted her with the fact that she would be well within the bounds of scriptural principle if she let him go. "I want you to read what the Bible says about marriage," I urged her, handing her a list of passages. "And I want you to pray. Maybe giving him up is for the best."

Now, as she sat before me, I could tell she had not taken my advice. "Did you read the verses I gave you last time?" I demanded.

"Yes," she replied. "And I prayed," she added before I could ask her.

"And?"

"And I really don't think God wants me to give up on this," she said. "God showed me that He is going to bring Jim back home. I know this isn't the answer for everybody, but I really feel God wants me to hang on."

I shrugged, not knowing what to say or do. If God had told her not to give up on Jim, how could I argue?

The situation grew even more grim. Before long, Jim divorced her. "Don't let it drive you crazy," I told her again. "Walk away from it and get on with your life."

She looked at me for a moment, and her eyes filled

with tears. Then she spoke with more determination than ever: "I will not give up. I will not let that woman destroy him. I will not let him destroy himself."

Annette did indeed stand firm. We prayed and talked together frequently. Others joined her in prayer. Then one day, incredibly, Jim's seven-year affair ended. Annette stepped in and helped him pick up the pieces of his shattered life. The thread that had held them together—because she refused to sever it—was stronger than ever.

One sunny Sunday afternoon, I had the privilege of remarrying Jim and Annette. And I thank God that she did not listen to my advice. She had repeatedly been forced to sift through the conflicting messages: "Give up." "You deserve better than that." "You have every right . . ." They were rational voices. They were compassionate voices. But they were *wrong* voices, and mine had been one of them.

Annette chose instead to listen to *God's* voice; she chose to care for Jim, God's child, despite his actions.

Annette is an ordinary woman, yet somehow God gave her the extraordinary patience and endurance to hang on through all the pain, the fear, the rejection, the agony that comes from watching a husband walk away. Annette was not perfect. At times she lashed out in anger and frustration. Yet, because she heard God and allowed Him to use her in her weakness, she saved Jim's life. Today the family is back together, and Jim is a deacon in their church.

What Annette demonstrated might be called "survival faith"—the faith that goes beyond the ordinary.

She had the faith that not only remembers the call of God but sinks its teeth into that call and refuses to let go for any reason whatsoever. In spite of advice. In spite of appearances. In spite of circumstances. In spite of all manner of torture.

Survival faith is not the domain of the strong and mighty. It is the domain of mature believers who love God and completely turn their lives over to the leading of the Lord. This kind of faith will come to any Christian in a time of crisis—and indeed it is the kind of faith that *must* come if the Christian is to survive the crisis points of life.

Puncture!

Sadly, many believers arrive at the inevitable crisis points of life without the foundation on which survival faith must stand. A young bull on the Mexican border taught me a lesson about survival faith in a vivid and unusual way.

El Paso is a city that enjoys an ongoing relationship with the people and the culture of Mexico. As one who was active in the media and in church circles, I made a variety of fascinating acquaintances both in El Paso and across the Rio Grande in Ciudad Juarez. One of the most interesting people I met was a young bullfighter named Fabian Ruiz. At twenty-two years of age, his reputation was growing rapidly.

The staff at the television station talked about producing a documentary special about Fabian, and in the process of discussing the possibilities, Fabian and I became good friends. As I grew closer to Fabian and his friends, most of whom were also matadors, they gave me a friendly challenge: I should train with them, they said, and experience the thrill of bullfighting. I was too intrigued to decline.

Day after day, I stood in the sun and the sand at the Plaza Monumental, the huge bullring in Juarez, learning the movement and motivations of the matador—the passes, the use of the cape, the danger signs. And at night, I practiced at home. Shirley quickly got tired of this.

But the practice paid off. Soon the matadors scheduled me for a *tienta* (tih-YEN-tah), the event where the young animals are tested for bravery. If they showed the killer instinct at this stage, they were sent to the ranch for breeding. I did not point it out to my matador friends, but I knew this *tienta* was going to be a test of *my* bravery too.

"You are ready," one of the matadors declared.

I was not so sure, and Shirley was even less sure. She thought the idea was dumb and dangerous. Finally, however, she and I agreed that I could not pass up a unique opportunity like this. How often in life do you get to be a matador?

On the day of the fight, I nervously stood behind the barrier, fending off anxiety while Fabian gave me last-minute instructions.

"My friend," he said, "there are two most important things to remember. First, when you step before the bull, plant yourself and do not move. Fear will try to force you but do not yield."

Easy for you to say, I thought.

"The bull will charge anything that moves so the cape must be the only thing moving."

I mumbled tensely that I understood.

"Second," he continued, "remember the *querencia*. You must not forget the *querencia*."

I remembered the word from my training. The *querencia* (keh-REN-see-ah) is the bull's "zone of safety," the area in which the bull feels safe. The moment he is released into the arena, the bull instinctively creates a *querencia*. He thinks that, because the few square yards around him are unthreatening at the moment, they will always be so. From that moment on, the bull will always feel safe within that area and unsafe outside of it.

For the matador the *querencia* is of paramount importance. For the bull it is a place of safety, but for the matador it is filled with danger. Because it is difficult to get the bull out of the *querencia*, the matador is often forced to go into the *querencia* after him. This puts the matador in close proximity to the bull, where he must now operate on the bull's terms.

Once the bull has moved outside the *querencia*, he becomes intensely uneasy and wants to return immediately to his space. The matador must not get between the bull and the *querencia* because the bull will charge whatever is in front of him. Many young bullfighters have ended up on the bull's horns that way.

With sweat beading on my upper lip, I mentally rehearsed all these pleasant tidbits of information and stepped into the arena.

I wish I could report that I was brilliant—a natural.

But it was not to be. I stood firm and dangled the large cape in front of the bull. He snorted and pawed the ground, then lowered his head and charged. The first two passes weren't too bad, but then on the third pass, I lifted the unwieldy cape up and over the bull's back and turned. The bull recovered much more quickly than I did, so I missed the next pass. The young bull scolded me by tossing me into the air. Fabian ran toward the bull with his cape and moved him away from me.

Embarrassed but determined, I picked myself up and tried again. This time I used the *muleta* (mu-LAY-tah), the smaller cape controlled by one hand. After a few successful passes, I felt my sense of dignity returning. Nevertheless, at the end of my caping with the *muleta*, I had left a strip of flesh from the side of my knee on one of the young bull's horns.

I immediately retired from my career as a matador.

The Mirage

The encounter left me with a bruised ego, a scarred body, and a profound lesson, which has stuck with me because I have seen it come to life hundreds of times since then.

The poor bull's tremendous security inside the *querencia*, the zone of safety, is futile. He imagines that he is safe there, but, ultimately, the *querencia* fails him. Sooner or later, his blood will stain the sand of the arena (if not when he faces Jerry Rose, then most certainly when he faces Fabian Ruiz!). The *querencia* provides false security, an illusion, which evaporates. It is no match for the matador.

We snicker at the bull's instinct for creating an imaginary zone of safety and his single-minded passion for reaching it; but people have *querencias* too. They feel safe or happy in some activity or pursuit and imagine they will always be safe and happy there. A little boy may dream of becoming a great civic leader. He imagines he will gain status and power and that such a life will make him happy. As he grows, he keeps his eye on that *querencia* and belligerently charges anything that comes between him and his goal. But even if he gets there, he finds that the *querencia* is not safe, and the dream-come-true does not fulfill him.

I have a friend who pitched for the New York Yankees. He was unhappy and restless, but he somehow came to the conclusion that he would finally have peace of mind if he could just pitch twenty winning games in a season. He accomplished his goal in 1970, thus reaching his *querencia*. But he was still restless and unhappy. Today he has found that happiness as a Christian.

I have seen the *querencia* mentality in career-minded people. They think the next elusive promotion will finally bring the fulfillment they long for. I have seen people whose *querencia* is financial security or material possessions. I have seen spouses in troubled marriages who think that happiness will come from a different partner. Each seeks a *querencia*—a mirage, an optical illusion that looks solid and secure. The bull finds out too late the truth about the *querencia*. Tragically, many people do too.

In that inevitable moment of crisis, when life crashes

in on you and your world explodes all around you, you will suddenly discover the worthlessness of your *querencia*, whatever it may be. When disaster strikes, when the doctor says "cancer" or the spouse says "I'm leaving" or the daughter becomes pregnant or when any one of a million other nightmares begins, *where do you turn?* What do you cling to? How do you survive?

That is the question of survival faith. And the answer is, once again, the *bedrock* of relationship with Jesus and the *inspiration* of His calling in your life. Jesus said in Matthew 11:28, "Come to Me, all ye who labor and are heavy laden, and I will give you rest." Without Christ, there is no survival faith.

So many have failed to understand this and have helplessly faced crises alone. They thought they could count on their job or their money or their lover. But they discover these to be only *querencias*. The true zone of safety is not in an executive office or a bank vault or a divorce court but within the arms of God. "Seek first the kingdom of God and His righteousness, and all these things shall be added to you" (Matt. 6:33). With this to stand on you can survive any crisis. You can know the strength and security of survival faith.

Is it wrong to pursue these other things? Of course not. But with survival faith you will gain proper perspective on career success, marital success, and other worthwhile goals. And as you learn to lean not on them but on the Father, you will be able to enjoy them to their fullest.

By the way, my friend with the Yankees eventually found Christ, the true *querencia*.

15

FIRE HAZARD

Survival faith has a bad reputation these days. Some have practically made an entire religion out of preaching a no-failure theology that simply does not relate to real life. These misguided folk will not admit that life sometimes becomes grim. But in fact, it does. Life will often cry out, "It's no use! Turn back! You can't make it!" Survival faith does not deny the hurt, the confusion, the pressure. Survival faith grits its teeth and replies, "Yes, it's dark, but I will go on because God is in control." Survival faith says, "Jesus loves me, and Jesus has called me, and as long as that's true, it doesn't matter whether I succeed or fail. All that matters is that I am His, and I am doing what He called me to do."

Meet Ken Dignan and you will get a dose of how tough life can really be and how powerfully survival faith can respond to it. Let me tell you his story backwards, starting from today. Ken is the successful pastor of a Chicago suburban church, which recently dedicated a brand-new sanctuary made necessary by their tremendous growth. Ken took the church when it was young and struggling. Before this, he served as an associate pastor in a large church and earned his masters in theology. In college he served as a dorm chaplain, influencing and counseling many young people. He finished his undergraduate studies at a Bible college, where he was valedictorian and Phi Beta Kappa. Several years ago, I had the privilege of nominating Ken for an achievement award, and by the time I finished filling out the form, I was awed all over again by this man's tenacity—physically, academically, and spiritually.

Ken contracted polio at the age of fourteen months. He was one of many victims stricken in the late 1940s and early 1950s, before the Salk vaccine. The disease left Ken partially paralyzed from the neck down.

"They thought I was going to die," Ken said of his childhood. "But I fooled them. I guess I was tough even then. From ages two to ten I had four surgeries to reduce my deformities. I had a traumatic childhood. My head looks like a mine field, it's so full of scars. I would try to run, ride a bike, or slide and end up falling on my head."

Ken's parents refused to treat him like a handicapped child. "My dad was a football coach," Ken recalled, "and he instilled in me a drive to keep going, no matter what. He taught me that it's not how bad something that happens to you is but how you react."

In school Ken was often left alone by the other children when they went out to play. "I was an outcast, a fire hazard, a nuisance some healthy kid might trip over in an air raid or fire drill." And as an adult, Ken lives in constant pain. He can't tie his shoes, dress himself, get out of a chair unassisted, or climb stairs.

FIRE HAZARD

"What changed your life?" I asked Ken.

"Music was the first thing," he answered. "In the eighth grade I learned I had an aptitude for music. I'd been listening to the Beatles and other sixties music. I had rhythm.

"My parents finally conceded, after a year of listening to me plead, and bought me a set of drums. With limited use of my hands, I couldn't ride bikes or horses, I couldn't swim or run, but I could play drums!"

Ken sank his life into this wonderful newfound outlet. "I got caught up in the rock music and the hippie culture. As a vent for my unhappiness and my limitations and because of my great need to be accepted by my peers, I grew my hair long and dabbled in marijuana and alcohol. I never liked the stuff, but I wanted so much to be part of a group."

Then one night Ken took some LSD.

"It gave me a bad trip," he remembered, "and for a long time I suffered from flashbacks, paranoia, anxiety attacks. At twenty, I quit the whole scene: the music, the friends—everything. I was afraid to go out. In my fear and torment I cried out to the God I remembered from my Catholic upbringing."

God responded to that cry. A Christian named Mark, heavy into the Jesus movement, had seen Ken perform with a rock group. He visited Ken and told him about Jesus. "After I had spent all my arguments and given all my excuses," Ken said, "I accepted his invitation to go with him to Bible study and church."

"Not long after that, I knew this was my answer. Jesus loved me; nothing else mattered. I couldn't get enough of the Bible stories and verses. It was such a relief to know I didn't have to struggle all by myself. I could feel God saying, 'Ken, you can't make it on your own. But I'm here to help you.'"

Ken Dignan, clinging to the bedrock of a relationship with Christ and building on the inspiration of that personal word from the Lord, began to exercise survival faith every day of his life. The Lord did not heal him physically. Some who fail to understand the reality of faith have quizzed him about that: "If your faith is so strong," they ask, "why haven't you been healed?"

"I don't know," Ken says. "As far as my body goes, I've had enough healing oil dumped on me to start a refinery. But the physical healing is not what matters. I have been healed in my spirit.

"Like Job, I have to say, 'Even though He [God] slay me, yet will I trust Him.'[1] I don't spend a lot of time worrying about why I'm not physically healed. I don't give up, but I have to agree with the apostle Paul in Corinthians when he tells of Jesus' promise: 'My grace is sufficient for you, for My strength is made perfect in weakness.' Then Paul explains, 'When I am weak, then I am strong.'"[2]

Ken Dignan could have chosen bitterness, tears, and self-pity. But instead, he has chosen life. He has chosen to submit to God, to obey Him, to trust Him regardless of the circumstances. Today Ken Dignan is a tower of faith. He has been through much deeper valleys than I have ever known, but Ken has survival faith because He knows a faithful God. "The name of the Lord is a strong tower; the righteous run into it and are safe."[3]

16

SUSTAINED IN THE VALLEY

Survival faith is not just for crises, nor is it necessarily characterized by tears and clenched fists and demonstrations of emotion.

I interviewed a husband and wife missionary team on "Among Friends." Former businesspeople, they went from upper-middle class to mud huts. Often they spent days tracking through the jungle to reach primitive tribes—from their descriptions, a tough life. Yet, they were saying things like "Praise God!" "God's grace is sufficient!" "The Lord really blessed us!" They had big smiles on their faces and acted as though they had enjoyed every moment.

"Overall, I have no doubt that God did bless you," I finally said. "And I'm sure you have found fulfillment. But you've come through some pretty rough times." I turned to the woman. "Most women need a sense of security and a home. Didn't you ever get discouraged?"

She looked sharply at me. Her smile disappeared, and she glanced down.

"Yes, there were times," she said quietly. "Times I

hurt so bad I didn't know if I could make it from one day to the next."

The real story was not that they had leapt from one glorious mountain top to another, continually praising God. The real story was that God had sustained them in the valley. They had suffered hurt, anxiety, discouragement. They had trudged through mud and rotting jungle vines, wondering at times where their next ounce of strength would come from. Yet they continued; despite their circumstances, they stuck it out.

When the inspiration withered, when it didn't feel good anymore, they stayed because God had called them there. That is survival faith. Survival faith is often invisible, deep beneath the surface. Survival faith can be mundane, like the discipline of bedrock faith, or the remembering of inspirational faith, long after the thrill of the inspiration has worn off. Survival faith means cheerful faithfulness even in the face of unpleasant circumstances. Survival faith means daily faith maintenance. You keep showing up so that God can use you.

Invisible Faith

Connie, a woman who works in the accounting department at TV–38, has demonstrated this crucial principle in her life. Raised in a churchgoing family, she learned to love Jesus like a friend when she was only a child. In her early twenties, Connie went to work in a bank, fell in with a non-Christian crowd, and adopted their habits. Eventually, she tired of the scene; and when she and her husband moved to the Chicago area, she took the opportunity to plunge into church work, ministering to young people, teaching Sunday school. "I was happy again," Connie recalled, "because I really liked that life so much better than the other one."

But life did not stay sweet. In a financial crisis, Connie and her husband lost their business, and their home soon followed. Their two teenagers were experiencing serious problems, and Connie's parents began to lose their health. Connie's father suffered from Alzheimer's disease, and her mother from Parkinson's disease. Connie took her parents into her home as their health deteriorated. To cover their demanding schedule, Connie worked nights and her husband, days—each caring for the elderly couple between shifts.

About this time I met Connie; she had taken a job at TV–38. Within two months, her husband, just sixty years old, died of a heart attack. Before long, Connie's father passed away. She still cares for her elderly mother.

Is Connie a grim-faced, sullen, bitter woman? Just putting that description on paper makes me smile because Connie is so completely opposite. She is a delight. She is a sunbeam—one of the cheeriest, most joyful people I have ever known.

She does not deny that the valleys have been dark. She has had a difficult life. But she has survival faith— the quiet, determined type. And with that faith, she has survived without the slightest trace of bitterness.

"Sometimes bad things happen," Connie admits. "My mother is now in the advanced stages of Parkinson's. We've had a lot of financial problems. Things aren't easy. But all the while, God keeps showing us that He's with us, He loves us, and cares about us."

Connie is not the model of perfection. "I won't say that there haven't been times when I've complained and asked, 'Why is this happening, God?'" she admits. "Then I remember, God isn't doing it to me. When life gets the very darkest, I think of what God says in His Word that He 'will not leave you nor forsake you.'"[1]

Connie stands firm on the bedrock. Prayer and Bible study are still priorities with her. "I talk to God like He's my friend," she says with a big smile. "Sometimes I look at the sky and say, 'Oh God, You did a beautiful job on the sky today.' Or, 'I'm really glad You're alive and You're working in my life!'

"I talk with Him like He's right there with me. Just like I'm talking to you! In difficult times I say, 'God, You've got to help me, 'cause I just can't see the top of it right now.' And He always does. If people would only realize how fulfilling it is just to know God like that!"

Connie is no deep theologian. She is an ordinary Christian woman who simply has an extraordinary relationship with Jesus.

"Have you ever had a friend you knew was there whenever you wanted him?" she asks. "And you could call any time of the day or night? You could ask the silliest questions, and he would answer? Well, that's God to me. God is that kind of friend. He's a better friend than any human being has ever been."

What a challenge—to cultivate that kind of relationship with the Father, banking on it when crises come and maintaining a sweet, Christlike spirit through it all!

17

GRANTED

I cannot say that I have always been as calm and sweet-spirited as my friend Connie, especially in the early days of my ministry with TV–38. After the Lord stunned me by bringing me to Chicago, I had to struggle with enormous conflicts in my spirit, as I watched this tiny, helpless ministry being born. By God's grace, the handful of dedicated Christians called to the work had just enough survival faith between them. When one of us ran low, the others seemed to make up for the lack. But there were many days when it was all I could do to hang on and keep hanging on.

I saw discouraging signs from my very first day. My "office" as vice president and general manager consisted of a battered wooden desk situated in a corner of the choir room at The Stone Church in suburban Chicago. I had no personal telephone but, instead, made my calls on whatever phone I could find unoccupied. For a staff car, I drove my 1966 Mustang. My briefcase served as a file cabinet.

Most disorienting of all was that I was vice president of a television station which had no channel and no license to operate. Owen Carr had signed a contract with the Chicago Federation of Labor (CFL) to purchase the never-used Channel 38 from them, but in order to buy the rights to the channel, we would have to be granted a license to operate the station within six months of signing the contract. No simple matter: a license must be approved by the Federal Communications Commission in Washington, D.C., a process involving volumes of complicated paperwork and long months of bureaucratic this-and-that.

"It doesn't look good for us," I grumbled at the end of another long day of wrangling with government officials. "The FCC says we need another four hundred thousand in cash or contracts for programming before they will issue the license." They wanted to make sure we could afford the transmitter before they would approve us to go on the air.

"Just between us," Shirley asked, "what are the chances of getting the money together?"

"Not good," I admitted. "We need a miracle. We've raised about two hundred and fifty thousand of it, but we've run out of resources and people. It seems impossible to raise one hundred and fifty thousand in the time we have left. Without God it will never happen."

Owen, ever faith-filled, sent me to Washington the next day to urge the FCC to grant us a license on the basis of the money we had already raised.

"Who knows?" Owen said. "Maybe we can wring a miracle out of the United States government."

"Fat chance," I muttered. I had dealt with government agencies one too many times before, but I agreed to give it a try.

In Washington I went straight to the office of Mort

Berfield, the lawyer we had hired for our dealings with the FCC. "Did you get the money?" he asked cheerfully.

I sighed and slumped into a chair. "Not enough. I came up here hoping to persuade them to give us the license anyway."

Mort's face changed. "No way," he said. "I've dealt with the FCC for years. Unless you have the money in hand or at least viable contracts, they won't grant the license."

In that instant, without warning, a flash of faith surged through me. I had never experienced anything like it before.

"Mort, the money will come in," I declared, confidence pulsing through me. "I have no idea how, but it will be here."

Mort arched his eyebrows and he shrugged—an "I-doubt-it" look.

"This is Monday," he said, glancing at his executive calendar. "Looks like you've got till four-thirty on Friday. You realize, don't you, that even if you get the money, it will take *days* to process the paperwork involved with this thing?"

I had nothing to say. I knew it looked impossible. I excused myself and called Owen. As I laid out the entire bleak picture I almost forgot the flash of inspiration God had given me.

"We'll expand our search for funds," Owen said emphatically. "I'll call more pastors and urge them to make commitments on behalf of their churches. You can try some of the Christian program producers around the country. See if you can secure commitments from them to contract with us for airtime."

I was astonished. "Owen, how can I ask them to advance us money and commit airtime when we don't even have a station?" I asked. "Or even a license?"

Owen's answer was another question: "Do you have any better ideas?"

I bade him a befuddled farewell and hung up. Discouragement was growing inside me. For that one brief moment, I had felt that God could do it, but now it just felt like the deadest of dead ends. Satan was doing everything possible to keep TV–38 from being born; I could see that. But what was *God* doing to bring the baby ministry into the world? That I couldn't see.

Grasping for help, I mentally searched the Word. And suddenly, Proverbs 3:5 broke into my mind: "Trust in the Lord with all your heart and lean not on your own understanding" (NIV).

Adrenalin Surge

Pow! I was rocked back on my spiritual heels. This verse blasted through me—heavy scriptural artillery. Instead of trusting God, instead of looking at His omnipotent possibilities, I was looking at all the human impossibilities. "In all your ways acknowledge Him," the passage goes on to say, "and he will make your paths straight" (v. 6).

A lifetime of knowing and trusting God had been all but obliterated by a seemingly overwhelming problem. But now, as I clung to the God I knew—the all-powerful God who had undeniably called us to launch a Christian television station in Chicago—I began dialing the phone with fervor. I would sell airtime on a station that did not exist because God was absolutely in this thing.

I called Vicki Jamison, a Dallas-based minister with a nationally syndicated television program. Years before, I had helped Vicki get her ministry started. Unfortunately, she couldn't help us, but she did recommend that we talk with Marvin Gorman in New Orleans. Marvin was an old friend, who had officiated at my wedding. I dialed his number.

"I would love to put the program on the air in Chicago," he said in his trademark gravelly voice. "And we'll lend you twenty-five thousand if you need it for your first year of operation."

Stunned, I thanked him and hung up. Immediately, I picked up the phone again, and dialed Gerald Derstine of the Christian Retreat in Bradenton, Florida.

"Sure, Jerry," he responded warmly. "We'll commit to twenty-one thousand dollars of airtime."

Now the spiritual adrenalin was pumping. I dialed Jack Wyrtzen's Word of Life ministry in Schroon Lake, New York. They contracted to buy a thirty-minute weekly time slot; we added another twenty-five thousand to the growing total.

Every call produced another contract! Only God could have given me such results.

Within a few hours, we had a complete program lineup and one hundred and seventy-five thousand dollars in commitments. Of course, we still had no television station, but who was I to argue with the God of survival faith?

Tuesday morning I could hardly wait to get into Mort's office.

"We've got twenty-five thousand more than we need," I gloated.

"Cash?" he asked.

"No, contracts," I answered. "Airtime commitments."

He frowned. "The FCC will have to check every detail of every applicant's status. I have a hunch most of these will be disqualified."

My jaw tightened. "It's all we have."

"Well, I'll do my best to get it through."

On Wednesday morning Mort and I sat in an office at the FCC with an FCC official and an agency accountant shuffling through the reams of paperwork. I prayed silently, feverishly.

The accountant looked over the first application and shook his head. "We can't accept this."

A knot tightened in the pit of my stomach. If the official agreed with him, the contract would be disqualified. *Please God*, I prayed silently, *somehow these have to go through!*

The official glanced over the application. I held my breath.

"It looks fine to me," he said casually, signing the release form.

The accountant was already looking skeptically at the next application. He disapproved it, but again the official overrode him. Over and over again the pattern repeated itself. I kept praying—pleading and praising, pleading and praising—until the two FCC men had approved more than one hundred and fifty thousand dollars in pledges!

Mort and I headed for the elevator; Mort was in shock.

"I don't believe it," he said, shaking his head at the miracle he had just witnessed. But then reality intruded again. "Don't count your blessings, though. This thing is far from over. It usually takes two weeks from this point for the FCC to process the paperwork."

"Two weeks!" I exclaimed. "But we've only got *two days* before our contract expires!"

"I know," he shrugged. "I'll see what I can do to hurry them up."

Jury Duty

Back in Mort's office, he phoned the FCC processing department. It was a short conversation.

"You're not going to believe this," he said, hanging up. "The guy who's been assigned to your case is out for jury duty."

I exploded.

"Jury duty!" I yelled. "What do you mean, jury duty? Government officials shouldn't have to do jury duty, especially not now!" I sank into a chair. "We're down to the wire on this thing! Can't they assign our application to someone else?"

Mort shook his head. "One thing I've learned is, you can't tell the government how to run their business."

I groaned. Wednesday was slipping away. I insisted Mort get on the phone and try to move the mountain. The FCC informed him they would see what they could do. That was all. Wednesday was history.

On Thursday morning I returned with trepidation to Mort's office. My hand was still on the door when his scowl stopped me cold.

"An agency official feels we're pushing the FCC too hard," he growled.

I tried to keep a lid on my anger. "What now?"

"We sit tight and wait," Mort answered. "I doubt anything will happen before four-thirty today. They assured me they would call as soon as they have an answer."

I stared incredulously at the lawyer. He shrugged helplessly. We had done our best. I knew the rest was up to God.

I left—no sense in hanging around. I walked the streets of the capital city, and I prayed. *Lord, it's in your hands. I don't know what else to do.*

Then, suddenly, He brought to my mind that same passage of Scripture He had given me on the day He first called me to Chicago: "No longer will you need the sun or moon to give you light, for the Lord your God will be your everlasting light."[1] Once again I was filled with that inexplicable feeling of calm. I knew that I could trust God no matter how insurmountable our situation seemed. God was in control.

Determined to relax, I did the "tourist thing" for the rest of the day: I visited the Smithsonian and the National Archives and had a wonderful time. Every two hours I called Mort for an update. Nothing. I urged Mort to try to phone the FCC again. He resisted. "No sense ruffling their feathers," he advised. "It could only hurt us at this point."

Friday morning. Our "D-Day" was here. Either we

came up with a license or the contract to purchase Channel 38 would be cancelled. I walked into Mort's office and pressed him to call the FCC again.

Reluctantly, he picked up the phone. The conversation was far too brief. He hung up. "They're working on it," he reported, "but they won't guarantee anything."

Understatement

I felt like a time bomb. I sat in Mort's office. I tried the pale blue velvet chair, then the pastel floral chair. After a while I moved to the couch, which turned out to be too small for napping. I paced the carpet. I read all the magazines in the office, even the outdated ones. I circled from the coffee pot to the bathroom down the hall and back again—several times. At noon, Mort and I went to lunch, then returned to the terrible task of waiting.

I wandered the halls of the office building and finally ventured out for a walk. My mind was so full of the FCC, Owen Carr, and TV–38 that, to this day, I cannot remember where I went. At three-thirty, however, I was again standing in front of Mort's desk.

"Did they call?"

Mort nodded. His face was a maddening blank. No joy. No sadness.

"Well, what did they say?" I demanded nervously.

Mort did not answer. He handed me a blue "While-You-Were-Out" note. I read the handwritten scrawl: *Chicago has been granted.*

The simplicity of the message, after so much complicated agony, struck me funny, and I erupted into laughter.

"This," I exulted, holding up the note, "has got to be the understatement of the century!"

Mort was too exhausted. He did not find it funny at all.

I grabbed Mort's phone and dialed Owen's number. When Owen heard my voice, he took a long, deep breath.

"Have you heard anything?" he asked. "I've been sitting by the phone all day, waiting for you to call."

I couldn't resist having some fun. "Yes," I responded in a deadpan voice. "We've gotten the word."

Owen paused a moment. "Well, what is it?" he finally demanded. "Look, Jerry, even if it's bad, I can handle it. Whatever the answer is, I've got to know."

Mort was watching me, amazed. "I can't believe this," he muttered, grabbing the phone out of my hand. He pulled it up to his mouth and shouted with glee: "We got it, Owen! *We got it!*"

A scant two hours before the deadline, Chicago had been granted. God had indeed wrought a miracle out of the United States government. Chicago had just been granted a full-time Christian television station.

We had survived—by faith. Owen Carr's enormous charge of survival faith had kept the fire flickering within me and taught me, once again, the lesson of the *querencia*. Once more I saw how frail every human plan really is and how totally trustworthy our faithful, omnipotent Father is. There had been no one to turn to; no one could take credit for this victory. We could only rely on God and cling to His character by a sheer act of survival faith.

But He, as always, had provided. Hallelujah!

18

COUNTDOWN TO CATASTROPHE

It should have been smooth-sailing after the difficulty of obtaining our license, but we would have even greater need for survival faith in the days ahead. With the channel now in our hands, we needed a studio and an enormous quantity of expensive technical equipment in order to broadcast. We counted on an outpouring of gifts from enthusiastic Christians all over Chicago, but instead of a flood, we saw only a pitiful trickle. Since we didn't have the money to buy equipment, Owen agreed to lease studio space, equipment, and crew from the Catholic Television Network. All we had to do was connect an underground line to carry our television signal from the Catholic Television Network studios on Wacker Drive over to our transmitter atop the John Hancock Building, a process that could happen by way of a simple call to the phone company.

We made verbal agreements with the CTN management while lawyers prepared the final papers. Meanwhile, we announced with great excitement that we would sign on the air on Memorial Day, May 31, 1976, at 5:30 P.M. We sent out press releases, designed and constructed sets, ordered programs on videotape, and contacted all the local churches to have their people tuning in. Six days before our scheduled debut, I got a call from CTN operations manager Doyle Caniff.

"Something's come up," he said. "Cardinal Cody of the Chicago archdiocese just sent word that he has important national programming in the works. He says it will require the full services of our facility. He expressed his regrets but said to tell you your programming would have to be cancelled."

Doyle cleared his throat and waited for my response. After a few speechless moments, I finally vented my frustration.

"Do you realize what you've done to us?" I exploded. "This leaves us in a shambles!"

"I'm really sorry about this," he said quietly. "I know how much you and Owen were counting on us."

I knew Doyle was powerless, stuck with the job of bad-news messenger, so I said a hasty good-bye and headed for Owen's office. He and I prayed fervently over the next couple of days, and in between, we repeatedly tried to talk CTN out of cancelling our contract. But they would not budge.

Finally, after another fruitless discussion with the Catholic Network people, I delivered my prognosis to Owen.

"It looks like the bottom has dropped out. It's humanly impossible to get our station on the air by Monday."

"I understand your concern," Owen responded calmly, "but let's not forget how God came through for us in Washington. All this, hard as it is to believe, is

God's timing. We may be building a television station, but God is at work in *us*, building *faith*. I say we hang in there and keep trusting Him."

I was astounded. All my knowledge of television was now a curse for it told me that there was simply too much work to be done, too many loose ends to tie up in time for a Memorial Day debut.

"I don't know how it's possible," I said to Owen, trying not to sound irritated at his naiveté. "We would have to start from scratch."

"I believe God will put us on the air" was all he would say.

"Owen, the only way this station can go on the air Monday evening is to run a tape through your teeth and let people see the program in your eyes."

Owen's laughter broke the tension. I laughed too. We talked briefly about our next steps, and then Owen offered a parting word of encouragement. "We'll just have to keep trusting God."

God's Timetable

Leaning more on Owen's survival faith than my own, I reviewed the production facilities we had considered before deciding on CTN. Only one was still a possibility: Olympic Studios, a small production company housed in a dilapidated building west of the Loop, right on skid row. They had little to offer—not much equipment, not much space, and no clear "land line" that would allow the telephone company to carry our signal underground to our transmitter at the John Hancock

Building. Originally, we hadn't considered Olympic a viable option. Now, suddenly, they looked *great*.

On Friday, only three days before our scheduled Monday sign-on, Owen and I met with Bill Brackett, one of Olympic's owners, and their production manager, Bob Ford. Somehow we managed to negotiate the use of their studio and equipment without letting them see how desperate we were. From their perspective, we were a windfall—the biggest account to show up on skid row in a long time.

Then I told them we had to be on the air by Monday. Bill's mouth dropped open. "You've got to be kidding."

Part of me wanted to admit that it was impossible. But I didn't. By an act of faith, I spoke words I could hardly believe: "We intend to be on the air Monday. Can you do it for us? If not, we'll have to find another way."

Bill paused to think, then said, "We can have you on the air. It will be tough, but we can do it. There's only one problem: You won't be able to get a land line in for at least two weeks. This holiday weekend will delay things even more."

I looked at Owen. Without the line connecting the studio to the transmitter, we would have no way to broadcast. But Owen's eyes did not register defeat. They communicated the same steady message they always had: *We're on God's timetable.*

"Let's call the telephone company and see if they can get it in," he said.

Lex Young, our chief engineer, chuckled. "Go ahead and call. It will give them a good laugh to end their week."

Indeed, the Friday afternoon before a three-day weekend was not the best time to call the phone company for quick service. But I called anyway. When I got a job supervisor on the phone, Lex's prediction came true. He laughed.

"You're kidding, right?"

"We really need to get a line in," I pleaded. "We're scheduled to go on the air Monday evening. Isn't there anything you can do?"

The man hummed thoughtfully for a second. "Tell you what," he replied. "I'll send a man out today to look, but we can't possibly get a line installed until next week sometime."

It wasn't enough, but I thanked him.

Owen and I went back to negotiating the fine points of our deal with Olympic Studios. Soon the telephone lineman arrived. We explained our predicament to him, then left him to his work. He wandered around the building for a few minutes, then returned to us.

"Did you guys know there was already a line back there?" he asked.

"There couldn't be," Bill frowned. He knew every square inch of the place. "There must be some mistake. And if there is, it would be dead because the company who owned the building before us went bankrupt, and they cut all the lines when they took their equipment."

"I know a telephone line when I see one," the lineman answered, "and it's there."

Owen and I looked at each other. Was God mixing up another miracle?

Bill was already following the lineman, who was

headed toward the back of the building. The lineman lifted a heavy table forward and showed us a wire he had pulled out of the wall. A quick test with his volt ohmmeter told us the amazing truth: The line was live and ready for use. God had drawn us to the one place in Chicago where we could find a live land line to the phone company—a small, run-down facility on skid row!

Ridiculous

Within two hours we had a television signal to the John Hancock Building. We would be able to broadcast live and in color, but we still had a lot of work to do and desperately needed more equipment than Olympic had on hand. Our top priority was to purchase a time-base corrector, a sophisticated, complicated piece of machinery worth eighteen thousand dollars—not the kind of thing you find on the shelf at Radio Shack. Standard procedure called for placing an order and waiting three months for delivery.

Again, God did the impossible. In a flash of divine inspiration, Owen said, "Why don't we call Roscor?"

It was a ridiculous suggestion. If the largest electronics firms in Chicago required three months, what could a tiny company like Roscor do for us? But by this time, I knew better than to say the word *impossible* to Owen. I dialed the number.

"Sure," the manager responded casually. "We'll have a time-base corrector to you within the hour."

I hung up and took a deep breath. It was almost enough to knock the wind out of a jaded television veteran like me. God's timing was astonishing, maddening. I thought of Habakkuk 2:3: "But these things I plan won't happen right away. Slowly, steadily, surely, the time approaches when the vision will be fulfilled" (TLB).

Suddenly, I was awed. I was witnessing the fulfillment of a vision. At that moment, it was impossible not to trust God completely. I could almost feel faith expanding within me, knocking down the walls of doubt.

We flung ourselves into our task. Except for engineer Lex Young, TV–38 had no production crew, so the men from Olympic scrambled to help us gather freelance people from all over Chicago. Lex and I stormed through the next seventy-two hours like twin hurricanes—gathering and assembling equipment, laying and connecting cable, setting lights, and seeing to hundreds of other details that go into producing live television.

What we lacked in equipment we made up for in ingenuity. We had no film chain, for example, so we mounted a projector on a Ping-Pong table. To an onlooker, I am sure we resembled a Keystone Kops comedy. It should have taken four months to accomplish what we did over that holiday weekend.

On Monday afternoon, as the mayhem reached fever pitch, people began to arrive. Unbeknownst to me, Owen had invited friends to view our maiden telecast. We ended up with over one hundred guests in a room designed to hold fifty. Every minute or so we found ourselves bumping into another clump of human obstacles.

As the deadline ticked toward us, the tension, the panic, the confusion grew to an incredible final crescendo. In the final few minutes, I glanced around at our makeshift studio. We were not exactly running a tape through Owen's teeth and watching it in his eyes, but almost.

With the five-thirty launch only seconds away, someone grabbed Owen and pushed him into position in front of a camera. Another thrust a bulky microphone into one of his hands. In the other he clutched his Bible. Through my headset I heard the countdown: "Three, two, one—we're on."

TV–38 burst onto the Chicago airwaves with Owen reading Genesis 1:1: "In the beginning God created the heavens and the earth. . . ." With a lump in my throat, I thought, *And praise God, He just created TV–38!*

I watched Owen awkwardly turning the pages of his Bible while juggling the microphone. He talked about the miracle-working power of God, and no one could know more of it, in that moment, than those of us in that studio on skid row.

As he drew his message to a close, he turned to Isaiah 9:2 and read the stirring words: "The people who walked in darkness have seen a great light; those who dwelt in the land of the shadow of death, upon them a light has shined."

That night, TV–38 glowed with the light of the gospel and streamed into homes throughout the Chicago area. I watched it all with a tired body but a joyful heart, realizing that God is in control. I have learned, first-hand, another harrowing lesson of survival faith.

Yet even this would not be my last encounter. I would still have to stare eternity in the face and summon up survival faith on my own behalf.

19

MALIGNANT

You may get to a stage in your walk with Christ when you think you have seen it all, learned it all, and you have your faith neatly packaged into a simple formula. That is usually when everything explodes, when, once again, you must experience the mystery of God's ways and the necessity of survival faith.

I've been there. Only a few years ago, after TV–38 had been on the air for several years, I felt life was going beautifully. Shirley and I loved our home in the suburbs. Our boys were growing strong and healthy; Vanessa was a delight. We had an adequate income and good health. I thought I had faith all figured out. And I felt I had enough faith to handle anything. You might say I thought I had made it to the top of the mountain. But I was soon to plunge into the darkest valley of my entire life.

I had never suffered a recurrence of the brain tumor crisis. I rarely even caught a cold, and that suited me fine. I enjoyed working the long, hard hours of the fast-paced television ministry. I felt great.

One afternoon, I went to our family doctor for my

regular physical examination. I casually mentioned to him that I may have passed a small amount of blood through my bowel, and the doctor suggested that I submit to a colonoscopy, just to check things out.

I ignored his advice for a long time—or tried to. I had no compelling reason to rush in for such a test. I had no alarming symptoms. I felt fine. Still, I could not get the doctor's recommendation out of my mind. *Go have this thing done and get it over with*, I kept telling myself.

Then one morning I heard the startling news: President Ronald Reagan had cancer discovered during a routine colonoscopy. Taken aback, I immediately scheduled the procedure. Shirley and I had planned a three-week vacation—a rare interruption from my heavy ministry schedule but a much needed break. I decided to have the colonoscopy done on the Friday before we left so I wouldn't have to worry about it during the trip.

When I awoke from anesthesia, the doctor surprised me: "You had two polyps," he said. "One was quite small; the other about the size of a golf ball. I've taken them out, but we'll need to check them." He then advised me to delay the start of our vacation until Monday, when the test results would come back.

I knew very well what "checking them" meant: The physicians would be looking for cancer. But I tried to put the matter out of my mind. Saturday was a blur as I hurried to clear my desk at the office. I was actually pleased to be leaving a day late, because it gave me a quiet, relaxing day with my family on Sunday.

On Monday, the doctor didn't wait for me to call him; he called me.

MALIGNANT

"One of the polyps is malignant," he said evenly. "That means there could be more cancer in your colon. We'll need to schedule you for surgery right away."

I was stunned, and for a while, I couldn't assimilate the information. I was healthy. I was fine. But as minutes stretched into hours, the truth sank in. I had cancer.

Within a couple of days, I lay on an operating table, waiting for the anesthetic to lift me into the oblivion of sleep. I wondered what it would be like to wake up on the other side of surgery. What would the doctors and nurses say? What kind of expressions would their faces bear?

It seemed only seconds later when I awoke. My eyes gradually focused on two bottles hanging nearby, tubes running from them into my arm. My nose and throat burned. I shifted slightly and felt another tube running from my nose.

There's been a mistake, I thought. *I must be dreaming.*

I shifted again to relieve the strain on my back. Pain tore through my stomach. I felt the thick, bulky dressing on my abdomen. No, this was no dream. This was my pain, my surgery, my cancer. I could no longer deny it or wish it away.

My mind was swamped with questions. *Why me, God? How could this happen? I've been faithful. I trusted You.*

Had I somehow failed God? What grave sin had I committed to receive this kind of punishment? *Where are You, God?* I cried. But I heard nothing other than the footsteps of a nurse in the hallway.

God had always been there before. Yet now, in the

darkest night of my life, I could not hear His voice or feel His peace. Where had I gone wrong? Had I wasted my entire life serving a God who did not care? Satan was going to do his best to crush me spiritually.

The Front

I summoned my energies, determined to recover quickly. Even with the IV's, a nasogastric tube and drains, I was up on the second day, walking the equivalent of a city block. Every morning and evening after that, I held a pillow against my stomach to ease the pain as I walked ten blocks, determined to regain my strength and get out of there fast.

To the medical staff and my fellow patients, I was the congenial Reverend Jerry Rose. No one guessed that inside, I was aching, not only with the pain of surgery but with the rejection I felt from the God I served.

I put on the spiritual front. I showed the world that I was fine, thank you, just fine. I had lived in faith for a long time, and I still knew how to act the part. All I wanted was for the pain to vanish. I wanted to forget the cancer had ever existed and live happily ever after. But I confessed some of my deepest, darkest feelings when a pastor-friend, Reverend Steve Wright, visited me in the hospital.

"If I had more faith, maybe this wouldn't have happened," I said. "I feel like a failure, like I'm no good to God anymore."

The chaplain smiled. "I get the feeling you're trying

to be something you're not. You're not so bad the way you are. Don't try to be a superman. Just keep walking in the Lord; just be who you are."

Those simple words hit home with me. He was right. I had been trying to be the macho-Christian—like the hurting missionaries I had interviewed on the television program—acting out the role of what I thought a Christian in crisis should be. Steve will never know what his simple advice meant to me.

But the doctor's words were not comforting. As I left the hospital, he sent me away with a grim reminder: "You're not out of the woods yet. There's a chance it could come back. We don't know and won't know for a while."

As I returned home, I felt *short-term*, as if I didn't have much time left. I should have been joyful, but I could not get over my feelings of inadequacy. Every failure I had ever experienced, every weakness, every sin, paraded through my mind, judging and tormenting me. Again and again I called out to God: *Have You rejected me? Is my ministry over? God, help me!*

Then, one night, there was a change. It came, ironically, as I was watching Christian television. Suddenly, I felt a strong compulsion to pray. *What you are feeling is not from Me*, the Lord spoke to my heart. *It is from the spirit of the world.*

I walked to my bedroom, knelt on the floor, and began to pray. I set aside any fragment of machismo. I stripped myself of all pretention. I poured out my heart to my Lord.

God, I want to live. I want to raise my family. I want to

finish the work You've called me to do. But more than that, I want to be in Your will. I'm sorry, Lord, for doubting You. I do trust You—no matter what.

As I continued to pray and listen and wait before the Lord, I began to feel a supernatural warmth flowing all over and around me. I instinctively thought of that phrase from my favorite psalm: "You anoint my head with oil."[1]

In a single glorious moment, the stifling black curtain of doubt and fear fell away. For the first time since the diagnosis of cancer, my anxiety was gone. I felt long-term again. God knew what was going on in my life. I could still trust Him.

Did this mean I would be physically healed? No, that wasn't the point. I was learning Job's lesson: Even if I were dying, I would still trust Him!

In that wonderful experience, I felt as though I had gone through a dark valley surrounded by mountains of fear and disappointment. But somehow, with God's help, I had climbed over those obstacles. I felt faith rising up like a wellspring inside me, miraculously overflowing its banks! I was back at my bedrock—my relationship with Christ.

Not the End

The trauma wasn't over. A few months later, my doctor discovered another trace of cancer in the colon and located what appeared to be a mass on the liver. The colon cancer could probably be surgically removed, but cancer of the liver was something altogether different.

"If this means what I think it means," he said solemnly, "we won't even bother to operate."

I did not feel wonderful; joy did not flood my spirit. I did not praise God and thank Him for bringing this insidious disease into my life so He could strengthen my faith. However, this time my faith was intact. Months earlier when I had gone through agonizing despair, I had come away with a firm decision to trust Him, even if it meant losing my life. And I was going to stand by that, no matter what.

It was time for bedrock faith—standing firm on my relationship with the Lord.

It was time for inspirational faith—remembering God's call upon my life and His promise to give me His best.

And it was time for survival faith—clinging to Him in spite of every opposing force.

In the Garden

Jesus Himself faced a life-and-death struggle—a far more grave and horrible situation than I will ever know. As He prayed in the Garden of Gethsemane, not far from His disciples, He "began to be filled with horror and deepest distress."

> And he said to them, "My soul is crushed by sorrow to the point of death; stay here and watch with me."
> He went on a little further and fell to the ground and prayed that if it were possible the awful hour awaiting him would never come.

"Father, Father," he said, "everything is possible for you. Take away this cup from me."

Then Jesus added the crucial condition of His request: "Yet I want your will, not mine."[2]

As I stood before death's door, I could relate in some small way to that agony. I could finally know the grief in His spirit. Perhaps now more than ever before, I could understand the weight of those four destiny-changing words: "Your will, not mine."

For a solid week, I lived with the possibility that I had liver cancer. Finally, a CAT scan revealed the truth: The liver had been partially obscured by the colon, causing it to appear as a mass. I would need a second surgery. I lost fourteen inches of colon in the first operation, and I would now lose fourteen more, but this was good news compared to what I might have heard.

I awoke from this surgery with the same scene as before—the same bottles and tubes, the same pain. But this time the anxiety and despair were gone. I even had a sense of humor. When Shirley walked in, I advised her of my new status: "Grammatically speaking, I am now a semicolon."

I could laugh! My faith had gone through a greater battle than ever before and won.

Survival faith clings through despair, through feelings of isolation and rejection, through Satan's lie that God has evacuated the premises. Survival faith hangs on by the fingernails; it does not let go.

And finally, it sees the light.

20

THE TEST RESULTS

In the opening pages of this book, you took a little test. Perhaps your answers came back to mind as you traveled through the Negev with Trevor and me or experienced the thrill of inspiration along with Gideon or "gutted it out" through the storms of life with Annette and Connie and Owen and me.

Maybe your answers are different now from they were before we began this journey. Ask yourself once again, with test on the following page.

There are *still* no scores in this faith test. But I hope you now have new insight into your own spiritual character and your own spiritual potential. Just for a moment, look back with me at the road we've taken, and perhaps we can put *Deep Faith for Dark Valleys* into a capsule so the principles you need for daily living will be readily available to you.

• The mountaintops are for thrills, and the valleys are for growth. When trials come, look for growth.

• A personal relationship with Jesus Christ is abso-

	Always or very strongly	Sometimes or somewhat	Rarely or not much	Never or not at all
1. Do you believe in God?	☐	☐	☐	☐
2. Do you think you will go to heaven when you die?	☐	☐	☐	☐
3. Are you satisfied with your life?	☐	☐	☐	☐
4. Do you think God is satisfied with your life?	☐	☐	☐	☐
5. Can you tell when God is speaking to you?	☐	☐	☐	☐
6. Do you spend time daily in Bible study and prayer?	☐	☐	☐	☐
7. Do you believe your faith is strong enough?	☐	☐	☐	☐
8. Are you obedient to God?	☐	☐	☐	☐
9. Do you feel you are fulfilling God's will for your life?	☐	☐	☐	☐
10. Do you have total trust in God for every detail of your life?	☐	☐	☐	☐

lutely essential to any form of faith. A living, breathing friendship with Him is the bedrock of a healthy Christian life.

• Jesus loves *you*—not your performance, not your success, not your possessions. He loves you even when you fail. He loves you eternally.

• Because He loves you so unconditionally, you do not need to pretend that everything is O.K. when it really is not. Admit that you hurt when you hurt and that you fail when you fail. In those valleys, He will sustain you.

• Because you have eternal life in Christ, everything else in this earthly life becomes less crucial—physical health, material wealth, even family and church. These are worthy pursuits, but eternity with Jesus is infinitely more important.

• Every relationship grows or dies. Grow your relationship with the Lord by a lifestyle of prayer and Bible study. It requires discipline, but it is absolutely essential to the faith-walk.

• You must learn to hear from God, not just at the major milestones of your life, but every day.

• God's will is not mysterious; He wants you to live it, so He will make it clear to you.

• God will call you not according to what you are but according to what He sees in you.

• To hear God, you have to screen out conflicting voices, even friends and family who mean well.

• God's calling in your life will not necessarily relate to what you prefer or what others prefer for you. It might not be what you expect. It might be *exactly* what you most long for. It might be easy or difficult, logical or illogical, embarrassing or glamorous. None of these considerations are crucial; what is crucial is *absolute obedience* to that calling.

• Sometimes you will have opportunities that seem so good they must be from God, but only by praying and hearing from God can you know for sure. Do not be fooled by how something *looks*.

• God will often call you to minister in small ways to others, to become involved in their lives. This is perhaps the most common calling, and in many ways the most difficult and challenging calling, known to all Christians. But it is essential to the life and health of the body of Christ.

• After you hear from God, remember that calling. Long after the excitement of the call has worn off, after the drudgery has set in, after circumstances have become difficult, after surprising obstacles have cropped up in your path, the calling is still just as real and accurate as ever.

• You may not believe that God can really use you the way He tells you He wants to use you. You may suffer from low self-esteem, and you let this hamper your usefulness and diminish your vitality in the kingdom. Rewrite the story you tell yourself about yourself. If God calls you to do it, He can do it through you.

• Sometimes you just have to hang on. When those crises come, when those seemingly endless battles are raging, you must hang on to *God*. Not your career, not your possessions, not your family. Ultimately, they can collapse around you. But God's character is immutable; trust in *Him*.

THE TEST RESULTS

Is there a bottom line? If there is, it is this: *When you daily live in relationship with Jesus, He daily speaks His will for you. No matter what surprises come your way, He will fulfill His plan for you in divine detail.* This does not always result in success by the world's standard. If it did, your existence would be so shallow, and you would have few opportunities to learn and grow. I believe I can say with integrity and from experience that I am glad for the valleys, glad for the low times. I do not enjoy them, but I am grateful for what the Lord can do in my heart and life while I am passing through them.

Sink your faith down to the bedrock of God's character. Tune in to His inspirational voice. And when the lightning strikes, you will have the elements of survival faith already in hand.

NOTES

Chapter 2   Back to the Beginning
1. Tom Peters, *Thriving on Chaos* (New York: Knopf, 1987), 258–260.
2. Romans 6:16, TLB.

Chapter 3   Storms Around the Skyscraper
1. Romans 8:39.
2. James 4:14.

Chapter 5   The Voice
1. Psalm 1:1–3.
2. Richard J. Foster, *Celebration of Discipline: The Path to Spiritual Growth* (San Francisco: Harper and Row, 1978), 1.
3. Ibid.
4. Hebrews 6:12–13, TLB.
5. Exodus 32:1.

Chapter 6   Tuning Out, Tuning In
1. See 1 Kings 18.
2. James 1:5–6.
3. Thomas R. Kelley, *A Testament of Devotion* (New York: Harper and Row, 1941).

Chapter 11   Remember the Inspiration
1. Jerry Bridges, *The Pursuit of Holiness* (Colorado Springs: NavPress, 1978).

Chapter 13   Rewriting the Story
1. "Cut from the Rock," by James Payne, First Monday Music/Word, Inc. Copyright © 1985. Used by permission.

Chapter 15   Fire Hazard
1. Job 13:15.
2. 2 Corinthians 12:9, 10.
3. Proverbs 18:10, NASV.

Chapter 16   Sustained in the Valley
1. 1 Chronicles 28:20.

Chapter 17   Granted
1. Isaiah 60:19, TLB.

Chapter 19   Malignant
1. Psalm 23.
2. Mark 14:32–36, TLB.